Mil Mi-24
Hind Attack Helicopter

DAVID OLIVER

AMBERLEY

First published 2023

Amberley Publishing
The Hill, Stroud,
Gloucestershire, GL5 4EP

www.amberley-books.com

ISBN 978 1 3981 0670 3 (print)
ISBN 978 1 3981 0671 0 (ebook)

British Library Cataloguing in Publication Data.
A catalogue record for this book is available from the British Library.

Typeset in 11pt on 14pt Celeste.
Typesetting by SJmagic DESIGN SERVICES, India.
Printed in the UK.

Contents

Introduction

The late 1960s were marked by the escalating war in Vietnam and the ongoing Cold War. It was also the decade that produced one of the most iconic military helicopters: the Soviet Union's Mil Mi-24.

Dr Mikhail Leontyevich Mil formed his own design bureau to develop rotary-wing aircraft starting in 1948 with the small piston-engine Mi-1. In June 1961, what was to become the most widely deployed multirole transport helicopters in the world with more than 18,000 built to date, the twin-turboshaft powered Mil Mi-8, dubbed Hip by NATO, took to the air.

Having studied the success of the American Bell AH-1 HueyCobra armed attack helicopter in Vietnam, Mikhail Mil submitted a proposal to the Soviet defence ministry in 1965 for a combat helicopter capable of carrying eight fully armed infantry into battle, as well as providing close-air support (CAP) for ground forces.

It took more than two years to convince the Soviet military that concept was viable before funding was released in late 1967. It was designed for increased agility, achieved by a high ratio of power to weight, combined with extensive armour and protection against ground fire and able to carry an up to 1,500-kg (3,300-lb) weapons payload.

Using dynamic components and the two Isotov TV-2 free-turbine turboshafts of the Mi-8 for the first Mi-24 prototype, the main rotor was designed for higher g-loads but the airframe design and construction was totally new. Mikhail Mil supervised the basic design before handing over to deputy chief designer Marat Tishchyenko. A directive was issued on 6 May 1968 to proceed with the development of the twin-engine design and detailed work began in August 1968 under the codename Yellow 24. A full-scale mock-up of the design was reviewed and approved in February 1969. The first free flight of a prototype occurred on 19 September 1969, flown by test pilot German Alferov, four days after tests began on 15 September 1969 with a tethered hover. Mikhail Mil died in January 1970.

The two prototypes were eventually joined by ten developmental helicopters, which eventually culminated in evaluations beginning June of 1970.

The first production version, the Mi-24A, NATO reporting name Hind-B, built by the Progress Arsenyev Aviation Plane, formerly Factory 116, in Russia's Far East, had a large four-seat cockpit for pilot, navigator/gunner and forward observer, with access via two large left-side window, a forward one hinging upwards and a bulged rear one sliding aft. The main cabin had a large split door that opened above and below, the lower section having integral steps. It had a retracting tricycle landing gear. It was armed with a 12.7 mm gun on a universal mount aimed by periscope looking through the ventral turret and rocket launchers and bombs carried on four munitions hard-points on shoulder-mounted anhedral stub-wings.

By the time the Mi-24A entered limited Soviet Air Force service in 1972, nicknamed the 'Drinking Glass', design of a new version had begun with more powerful TV3-117 engines, a port-side tail rotor and the entire front fuselage redesigned forward of the engine air intakes. This comprised separate cockpits for the weapon operator with a bulletproof front screen, upwards hinged canopy with steps up the left side, and a higher rear cockpit for the pilot in tandem with access via a hinged door on the right.

Titanium armour was fitted under the floor, round the cockpits and protecting engines and gearbox with an anti-fragment panel between the cockpits, both of which had quadruple seals to provide a positive over-pressure system to prevent the ingress of chemical or biological agents. The Mi-24D, NATO reporting name Hind-D, was armed with a chin-mounted four-barrel 12.7 mm YakB machine gun, and longer stub-wings with six munitions hard-points for missile and rocket launchers.

The Mi-24 was one of those Soviet designs that clearly showed NATO that they were not simply copying Western ideas. The Soviets looked at their helicopter needs and came up with a unique solution, one that became feared on the many battlefields where it was deployed, while Mi-24 regiments of the Warsaw Pact (WarPac) countries were a constant threat to NATO war planners until the end of the Cold War.

The Mi-24D and the variants that followed it into service was called the 'Crocodile' by its aircrew due to the helicopter's shape and camouflage scheme.

To cope with demand, the Mi-24 was also produced by Rostvertol, the former Factory 168, at Rostov-on-Don from 1976 where its later variants continued to be manufactured for more than fifty years, with more than 3,500 built in thirty-five variants.

More than fifty years since its first flight, versions of the Mil Mi-24 are operated by armed forces of more than sixty countries worldwide, deployed to conflict zones in three continents, and continue in production, with new variants being developed, most of which will remain in service for decades to come.

Mil Mi-24V '70 Red', the Rostvertol gate-guardian at the Rostvertol factory at Rostov-on-Don since 2009. (David Oliver)

The view from a Mi-35P flying over Surrey's Redhill Aerodrome during the Soviet Hind's first flight in UK airspace in 1989. (David Oliver)

The latest variant of the Hind, the Mil Mi-35M multirole combat helicopter used for ground attack, assault and cargo transport. (Rostvertol)

Chapter 1

Development and Production

A trainer version of the initial Mi-24A without gun or rocket rails was produced in small numbers as the Mi-24U, dubbed Hind-C by NATO. One was adapted to fly without wing nacelles and modified main rotor to avoid vibration. Designated as A-10, it was used in 1975, when test pilots Galina Rastorgueva and Lyudmila Polyanskaya set eight FAI records for speed and lifting, including a speed of 334.464 km/h over 100 km and a time of 2 minutes 33.5 seconds to 3 km and 7 minutes 43 second to 6 km. Climb record included 2 minutes 33.5 seconds to 3,000 metres and 7 minutes 43 seconds to 6,000 metres. On 21 September 1978 Mil test pilot Gurgen Karapetyan recorded the highest speed by any helicopter, at 368.4 km/h in the A-10 fitted with TV3-117G turboshafts. This record stood until 1986, when it was broken by the current official record holder, a modified British Westland Lynx.

While the Mi-24A Hind-B was still in production, 240 of which were built, the extensively redesigned Mi-24D was being developed. It had a smaller 56 feet 9 inch (17.3 metre) diameter five-blade main rotor compared with the original Mi-8 rotor used on the first prototype. The leading edge of each blade had an anti-erosion strip and electrothermal deicing and a balance tab was fitted on the training edge. The three-blade tail rotor set on the left side of the fin was offset by 3 degrees.

The 57 feet 6 inch (17.5 metre) long Mi-24D had a streamlined all-metal semi-monocoque fuselage pod and boom and a 21 feet 10 inch (6.66 metre) wingspan. Stub-wings were set at a 12 degree anhedral and provided some one-quarter of the lift in cruising flight. The tricycle landing gear comprised a rearward-retracting steerable twin-wheel nose unit and single main wheel units that retracted rearward and inward into the fuselage pod.

Two 2,200 shp (1,640 kW) Isotov TV3-117 turboshaft engines were installed side by side above the cabin fitted with air intake vortex type dust/debris extractors. An AI-9W auxiliary power unit (APU) was installed in the rear of the rotor head.

The avionics of the Mi-24D included the chin-mounted low-light television (LLTV), laser designator/ranger and forward-looking infra-red (FLIR). A missile guidance pod was under the left side of the nose. HF and duplicated UHF VHS, ARK-UDR 852 radio compass and ARK-15M ADF, DISS-15D doppler driving roller-map pilot display were fitted. Duplicate RW-5 radar altimeters were under the boom and SRO-2 identification friend or foe (IFF) antennas above the front windscreen and under the tail. Odd-Rods radar warning receivers (RWR) were each side of the nose and on the tail. A large boom projecting ahead from the top of the front windscreen carried low speed precision sensors.

Armament included the chin-mounted 12.7 mm four-barrel YakB machine gun slaved to a KPS-53A electro-optical under nose sighting system with reflector sight in the front cockpit. In addition to UV-32-57 rocket launchers and GSh-23L twin barrel 23 mm gun pods, the Mi-24D was armed with four AT-2 Swatter, AT-3 Sagger or AT-6 Spiral short-range anti-tank guided missiles (ATGM) on six stub-wing pylons.

The Mi-24D was cleared for production at Progress Arsenyev and Rostvertol in 1978 at a rate of fifteen per month. A small number of a dual-control pilot trainer versions, the Mi-24DU, with the gun turret removed, were built before production switched to the Mi-24V in late 1980 after 635 Mi-24Ds were built. The Mi-24V, NATO reporting name Hind-E, could be armed with UV-20-76 rocket launchers and twin AA-8 Aphid air-to-air missiles in addition to anti-tank missiles.

A coded-pulse IRCM emitter was mounted on the rear end of the rotor-head fairing while ASO-2V chaff/flare dispensers initially fitted under the tailboom, later triple packs with a total of 129 flares, were fitted to the sides of the centre fuselage. A forward oblique fixed searchlight added to the nose and the combat camera moved to the left wingtip. A head up display (HUD) replaced the pilot's former reflector gunsight. A total of 309 Mi-24Vs were built at Progress Arsenyev and Rostvertol.

Experience of combat in Afghanistan (see Chapter 2) led to the Mi-24P variant's chin-mounted gun turret being replaced by a side-mounted GSh-30-2 twin-barrel 30 mm gun. Dubbed Hind-F by NATO, eighty-seven were built between 1980 and 1990. Other versions included the Mi-24K Hind-G2 equipped with a large camera in the cabin and a video/EO device with a 1,300 mm lens to the right of the nose turret. Six Mi-24Ks were issued to Soviet Army Aviation helicopter regiments for reconnaissance and artillery fire correction.

The Mi-24VP had a twin-barrel 23 mm GSh-23 gun and the Mi-24RKh, Hind-G1, was a special nuclear, biological and chemical (NBC) version with sensors and missile rails replaced by 'clutching hand' mechanisms on lengthened pylons to obtain soil samples for NBC warfare analysis. Air samples were sucked into the hermetically sealed cabin via a pipe on the port side and a datalink passed the findings to a ground station. Some 200 were built between 1983 and 1989, with six being deployed to Soviet Army Aviation helicopter regiments.

Sanitized export versions of the Mi-24D, other than those supplied to WarPac forces, were designated Mi-25 and the Mi-35 was the export designation of the Mi-24V.

In 2004 sixteen Mi-24PNs were ordered for the Russian Air Force equipped with the 9S47N Zarevo III electro-optical (EO) aiming system fitted under the nose. Two converted Mi-24Ps and twelve new-build helicopters from Rostvertol were fitted with short span stub-wings and fixed undercarriage developed for the next Hind variant, the Mi-35M.

The Mi-35M is a comprehensive update of the Mi-24V designed to meet the latest requirements of the Russian Army. They entered production at Rostvertol in 2005. All-weather day-night equipment includes an NEI-24 navigation system, a GOES-342 gyro-stabilised EO turret within its OPS-24N observation-sighting system and a PrVK-24 sight.

Powered by two 2.170 shp (1,618 kW) Klimov VK-2500-02 turboshafts with reduced noise levels and maintenance requirements, the Mi-35M has a maximum speed of 186 mph (300 km/h) and a cruising speed of 161 mph (260 km/h). They have a hover ceiling of 10,340 feet (3,150 metres) and a service ceiling of 18,050 feet (5,400 metres). The Mi-35M has a ferry range of 620 miles (1,000 km) with a combat radius of 400 miles (450 km).

Armament includes up to eight 9M114 Shturm-V or 9M120 Ataka-V ATGMs on four underwing hardpoints, and 80 mm S-8 series or 122 mm S-13 unguided rockets. Two UPK-23-250 pods containing GSh-23L 23 mm cannon and 250 rounds of ammunition can also be carried under the stub-wing assemblies while a twin-barreled GSh-23L 23 mm cannon is mounted in the chin turret.

It features a new composite five-bladed main rotor and X-tail rotor system, and the armament stub-wings had been shortened to help promote a reduced forward/rear profile. The Mi-35M has a fixed-wheeled tricycle undercarriage to improve its rough field operational capability.

The PSV (Future High-Speed Helicopter) demonstrator was a highly modified Mi-24K with an all-new nose section, new main-rotor blades and more powerful engines with a full digital authority control system. The maiden flight of the PSV took place on 29 December 2015 at Mil's flight test centre in Tomilino near Moscow. It subsequently achieved a maximum speed of 218 kts (403 km/h). The technologies tested on the PSV would be used in the design and development of a new generation of high-speed military helicopters and in 2016 it was fitted with straight long-span wings and new exhaust ports.

In 2020, Rostvertol launched an upgraded Mi-35P equipped with the OPS-24N-1L sighting system, a third-generation matrix long wavelength thermal imager, high resolution colour TV camera and a laser range finder. The helicopter also has 3+ generation NVGs with external and internal lighting equipment adapted for their use. A new digital flight control system provides automation to support the pilot.

The Mi-35P is armed with a GSh-30K twin-barreled cannon, S-8 rockets, and can carry underwing pods with 23 mm cannons, S-13 rockets, Ataka-V ATGMs and Vikhr-1M laser-guided missiles.

The Mi-24A, designated by NATO as Hind-B, entered service with the Soviet Air Force at Dredsen-Hellerau in East Germany in 1975. (Russian Helicopters)

Soviet Air Force Mi-24A '20 Red', preserved in Latvijas Aviacijas Tehnikas Muzejs. (Toma Milosch)

The first Soviet Hind to fly over England was Mi-24P Hind-F '11 Red', built at Arsenyev in 1989. (David Oliver)

Known in the Soviet Union as the Hunchback, the bulky Mi-24P Hind-F had a maximum take-off weight of 24.692 lb (11,200 kg). (David Oliver)

The Hind-F's stub-wings are able to carry up to 3,307 lb (1,500 kg) of weapons including four 80 mm S-8 rocket launchers and four AT-6 Spiral anti-tank missile launch tubes. (David Oliver)

The Mi-24RKh Hind-G1 was a special nuclear, biological and chemical (NBC) version. (Robert Schleiffert)

The pilot's analogue instrument panel of a Mi-24D Hind-D. (Mike1024)

The view from the weapons systems officer's front cockpit. (VTS)

A factory-fresh Mi-35M is prepared for a test flight at Rostvertol's airfield. (David Oliver)

The Mi-35M's armament includes 9M114 Shturm-V or 9M120 Ataka-V ATGMs, 80 mm S-8 unguided rockets. UPK-23-250 pods containing GSh-23L 23 mm cannon. (Rostvertol)

The PSV (Future High-Speed Helicopter) demonstrator was a highly modified Mi-24K that made its maiden flight on 29 December 2015. (Russian Helicopters)

In 2016 the PSV was fitted with straight long-span wings and new exhaust ports. (Russian Helicopters)

Chapter 2
In Soviet Service

The Mi-24A Hind-B saw only limited service with the Soviet armed forces due to problems encountered during its evaluation by the military. One was that hovering in a crosswind could result in the Mi-24A rotating uncontrollably on its vertical axis. After a number of accidents, the tail rotor was moved from the starboard side of the tail to the port side.

Combat doctrine was shifting and planners saw the Mi-24A increasingly as an armed troopship as the inadequacies of the AT-Swatter anti-tank missile rendered the Mi-24A redundant in the CAS role. It was retained mainly for aircrew training and tactics development. The first Mi-24As were identified in East Germany in early 1974, with two squadron strength units with the Soviet 16th Frontal Aviation Army.

The Mi-24 force was assigned to the Frontal Aviation arm of the Soviet Air Force, which was the Russian version of the Western tactical air force, organised into sixteen Tactical Air Armies. Soviet tactical doctrine at the time indicated that in the case of hostilities, the Hind regiments would be placed under operational control of front commanders for direct support of breakthrough operations.

A 1977 report by the US Army Institute for Advanced Russian and East European Studies estimated that the USSR had approximately 300 Hinds operational in three configurations: A, C and D models. The report also felt that Russia's helicopter production had increased over 50 per cent from predicted Pentagon estimates. It stated that rapid growth of the Soviet attack helicopter force could only be seen as their 'very real' belief in its ability as an element of success in the battlefield equation. NATO would do well to watch this progress closely for it could indicate the Soviet's perceived concept for the rapid tempo of the battlefield of the future.

Following the introduction of the Mi-24D into service, they took part in large-scale Soviet military exercises making simulated attacks on tank forces, while time was devoted to training riflemen to shoot at soft ground targets from the Hind's cabin windows. For anti-personnel area suppression missions the Soviet Air Force developed a strike element of three Mi-24s. The combat formation comprised two helicopters in a search and strike element while the flight commander's Hind flew above and behind to ensure good visual contact and mutual fire support. However, NATO observers familiar with this three-ship element would concentrate their defensive efforts on the rear helicopter, which could prove costly in a real war.

In the event, there was no real war between opposing forces of East and West in Europe. The first taste of combat would come in the remote battlefields of distant Afghanistan. In December 1979 the president of Afghanistan was murdered and a puppet government took over, who invited the Soviet Union to help crush any opposition by bringing in a small element of the Soviet army. Although the coup had been planned well in advance, what had been miscalculated was the determination of the Afghan people to resist. This eventually led to a massive build-up of Soviet forces with its Frontal Aviation playing a major role in trying to eliminate all opponents of the new regime. Apart from the Su-25 Frogfoot ground attack aircraft, the most numerous single type in the Frontal Aviation units deployed to Afghanistan was the Mi-24.

They were deployed to dislodge and disrupt rebel forces throughout the unforgiving Afghan terrain while being assigned to convoy escort and fire support missions as needed. To begin with the Hind proved very effective at pinning down the rebel Mujahedeen forces both by day and night and could unleash devastating fire against their caves and rock crevices with its gun, rockets and anti-tank missiles. Against an ill-equipped rebel force, the Mi-24 became the most feared single weapon deployed by the Soviet forces against the Mujahedeen, who called it the 'Devil's Chariot'.

However, several Hinds had been shot down by carefully aimed rifle fire, and its vulnerability was further exposed when the Mujahedeen were supplied with CIA-delivered FIM-92 Stinger short-range, surface-to-air missiles (SAM). At the time its complete lack of infra-red signature suppression had an adverse affect on its survivability in combat. A 1987 CIA report said that the number of Mi-24s in theatre increased from eighty-five in 1980 to 120 in 1985, many in Afghan markings, although most were flown by Soviet aircrew.

An aviation unit of KGB Border Troops based at Almaty was deployed to Gol Khaneh in Afghanistan with its Mi-24Ds in 1987. On 3 October two of its Hinds were patrolling the mountain passes in southern Afghanistan near the Pakistani border when visibility deteriorated and they strayed into Pakistani airspace. After landing to establish their exact position they tried to overfly a mountain range heading for Gol Khaneh, but ran out of fuel and landed 19 km south of the border. When Pakistani Frontier Corps Tochi Scouts approached the helicopters the crews surrendered without resistance on orders from the KGB Border Guard HQ, and were later flown by a KGB Border Guard An-72 to Dushanbe in Tajikistan, but the helicopters were retained by Pakistan, one of which was later handed over to China and the other to the United States.

Despite the large Soviet commitment to the war effort, it cut its losses in 1989 and withdrew its forces. The last loss of life in the war occurred when a Mi-24V was shot down by Afghan rebels on 1 February, its two crew killed. A total of seventy-four Mi-24s were reported to have been shot down by ground fire in Afghanistan. By the end of the Cold War two years later, the Soviet Army Aviation had a total of 1,420 Mi-24s on strength.

Limited numbers of Soviet Mi-24 Hind-Bs were deployed to East Germany in 1974. (Rostvertol)

Soviet Mi-24 Hind-Ds took part in large scale military exercises making simulated attacks on tanks formations. (DoD)

Soviet riflemen were trained to shoot at soft ground targets from the Hind's cabin windows. (Rostvertol)

Soviet Hind's first taste of combat was against rebel forces to the Afghan government in 1979.

Left: The Soviet weapon systems officer in the front cockpit of a Hind in Afghanistan armed with his Kalashnikov AK-47 for protection if shot down.

Below: Many Soviet Hind-Ds were flown in Afghan colours by Soviet aircrew deployed against the Mujahedeen, who called it the 'Devil's Chariot'.

Many Hinds in Afghan colours were flown by Russian pilots.

Engine filters were added to Soviet Mi-24Ds in Afghanistan to reduce ingression of dust and sand during operations.

Soviet Mi-24P Hind-F '07 Red' flying over Kandahar province in 1988.

CHAPTER 3

Warsaw Pact Operations

East Germany

Next to the Soviet armed forces the East German Air Force was the best equipped and most modern WarPac air arm. On 18 January 1956, the East German People's Army was established and work began on the formation of a new air force.

East Germany was also the first WarPac country to take delivery of the Rostvertol-built Mi-24D Hind. June 1978 saw the Hind-D introduced into the East German Air Force & Air Defence Force, with an initial delivery of four aircraft. The helicopters were regularly detached to forward helipads in order to provide quick-reaction protection for radar sites located near the West German border.

The East German Air Force had two regiments flying the Hind-D. The first was KHG-57 'Adolf von Lutzow', based at Basephol, whose crews were trained in the anti-tank role, and the second assault helicopter unit was KHG-67 'Ferdinand von Schill' based at Cottbus. The regiments operated a mixed fleet of thirty Hind-Ds and Mi-8TB Hip-Cs, plus a number of Mi-3 Hoplites for liaison and reconnaissance. An Mi-24 flight simulator was available for the Mi-24 pilots, which was another first for the East German Air Force. The helicopter regiments used several different designations during the Hind's service life but their final designations were KHG-3 at Cottbus and KHG-5 based at Basepohl at the time of the reunification of Germany in 1990. At least four East German Mi-24Ds had been lost in accidents.

With reunification of Germany in 1990 the separate air forces of the East and West Germany were united in the new Luftwaffe. The new Luftwaffe evaluated the Hind and it was briefly operated by two Germany Army Aviation squadrons, Heeresfliegerstaffel 79 and Heeresfliegerstaffel 80, before being retired from service. Some of the aircraft were sold to Hungary and Poland and two sent to the USA for evaluation purposes. One was donated to the United Kingdom's Imperial War Museum at Duxford. In 2012 this Mi-24D was loaned to the Pima Air & Space Museum in the USA.

Poland

In March 1947, the wartime Air Force of the Polish Army was renamed as the Polish Air Force, which would become the largest air force in the Eastern Bloc's Warsaw Pact (WarPac) nations, apart from that of the Soviet Union.

In September 1978 the first of sixteen Mi-24Ds were delivered to the Polish Army Aviation and were operational by January 1979. As there existed a WarPac-wide policy on the employment of attack helicopters, Polish Hind roles and operations were similar to those of other Eastern Bloc countries.

Between 1986 and 1991, sixteen examples of the improved Mi-24V Hind-E, Polish designated Mi-24Hs, that carried four AT-6 missiles were delivered. The Polish Army Aviation operated mixed fleets of helicopters, although most of the sixty Mi-24s in service at the end of the Cold War were with regiments based at Latkowo and Pruszcz-Gdanski.

Hungary

The new Hungarian Air Force was established in 1949 after the People's Republic of Hungary was declared a communist state and its first Russian helicopters, Mil Mi-1s, were delivered in early 1956 just prior to the Hungarian Revolution, which was supported by some air force officers. Before the uprising, the Hungarian Air Force was one of the strongest in the Balkans, but after it was suppressed by the Soviets it was demobilised.

Its rebirth in the early 1960s was under close Soviet control and having been established as a reliable WarPac partner, in March 1978 the Hungarian Air Force received its first of thirty Mi-24D Hind-Ds equipping one regiment and one mixed Mi-8/Mi-24 unit based at Veszprem. Ten upgraded Hind-Es were delivered and in 1988 equipped with 80 mm rocket launcher pods to replace the UB-32 pods for Type S-5 rockets. In 1991 a special detachment of Hind-Es, detached from Szentkiralyszabadja for border patrols, were based at Taszar near the Yugoslav border on twenty-four-hour alert when hostilities erupted.

Czechoslovakia

The Czechoslovak Air Force ordered a fleet of sixteen Mi-24Ds delivered between 1978 and 1983 as part of a modernisation programme. Given Czechoslovakia's proximity to the border with NATO, it received another twenty Mi-24Vs and an Mi-24DU trainer between 1985 and 1989 and the Plzen-Bory airfield became a front-line air base for Hind operations for any NATO/WarPac conflict.

On 12 September 1985 while on a patrol flight along the border with West Germany a Czechoslovak Mi-24 engaged in friendly air display manoeuvres with a US Army AH-1S HueyCobra in mountainous terrain near PráÜily and crashed due to a lack of performance in key areas of the flight envelope, injuring two of the three crew. Another three Mi-24s were lost in accidents.

Bulgaria

The air arm of the Socialist Republic of Bulgaria was one of the least known of all the WarPac air forces. It was surrounded by tight security that kept it isolated from the outside world. The extensive Sovietisation of the Bulgarian Air Arm led to the eventual change of its official title in late 1949, featuring a structure identical to that of a Soviet front-line air army.

A total of thirty-eight Mi-24Ds were delivered to the Bulgarian Air Force between October 1979 and 1985, plus six Mi-24Vs in 1986, and the type remained in service throughout the Cold War and beyond. The three main roles for Bulgaria's Hinds were in providing CAS for ground troops, anti-armour operations and battlefield air defence against slow-speed aircraft and helicopters.

A Combat Helicopter Regiment was formed in 1981 to operate the Mi-24Ds based near Stara Zagora in central Bulgaria. The Bulgarian Air Force had forty-four Mi-24s on strength at the end of the Cold War.

By 1988, it was estimated that there were some twenty WarPac regiments flying a total of 600 Hind helicopters and the regiments facing NATO across the inner German and Czech borders had full night-fighting capability in fire support, anti-helicopter and anti-tank roles. The mix of weapon systems including the continued use of unguided rockets with a range of 1.9 miles (3,000 metres) indicated the fire potential of the Mi-24. At the same time, the number of Hinds flying close to the borders was increasing and it was a weekly occurrence for border patrol flights of NATO helicopters to encounter Hind activity.

East Germany was the first WarPac country to take delivery of the Rostvertol-built Mi-24D Hind-D in June 1978.

Polish Army Aviation Mi-24V Hind-E belonging to the 49th Combat Attack Helicopter Regiment based at Pruszsz-Gdanski.

Mi-24Ds '487' and '434' assigned to KHG-5 'Adolf von Lutzow', based at Basepohl in the late 1980s.

Mi-24V '734' was delivered to the Polish Army Aviation in 1986 and operated by a unit assigned to the 56th Air Base at Inowroclaw-Latkowo.

The Hungarian Air Force operated a Mi-24D Hind-D regiment based at Veszprem.

Hungarian Air Force Mi-24+ '574' was delivered in February 1985 to the 86th 'Szolnok' Helicopter Base and withdrawn from service in 2011. (Aldo Bidini)

Czechoslovak Air Force Mi-24D 0222 was delivered in June 1982 and transferred to the Slovak Air Force in January 1993. (David Oliver)

A Czechoslovak Air Force Mi-24D lift off inches above the ground at Prague-Kbely Air Base with its large area exhaust seen against the tree line. (David Oliver)

Above: The rear veiw of this Czechoslovak Air Force Mi-24D shows its four UV-32-57 rocket launchers under the stub-wing and AT-2 anti-tank missile rails under the tips. (David Oliver)

Left: Czechoslovak Mi-24D '4012' that crashed near the West German border in September 1985 after mock combat with a US Army AH-1S Cobra.

Chapter 4

Middle East Operators

Iraq

More than fifty Mi-25s, the export version of the Mi-24D, were delivered to Iraq from 1978 and saw considerable use during its long war against Iran. However, the Mi-25s were only armed with obsolete AT-2 Swatter missiles, which led the Iraqis to develop new gunship tactics with help from East German advisors. The Mi-25s would form hunter-killer teams with French-built Gazelle helicopters, with the Hinds leading the attack and using their massive firepower to suppress Iranian air defenses, and the Gazelles using their HOT missiles to engage armoured vehicles.

The war also saw the first air-to-air helicopter battles in history when in November 1980, two Iranian SeaCobras engaged two Iraqi Mi-25s with TOW wire-guided anti-tank missiles, shooting one down and badly damaging the other. The Iranians repeated this action on 24 April 1981, destroying two more Mi-25s and another downed by an IRIAF F-14A Tomcat.

The Iraqis claimed the destruction of a SeaCobra on 14 September 1983 with the Mi-25's YaKB machine gun, then more in February 1984. It also claimed that a Mi-25 shot down an IRIAF F-4 Phantom using its S-5 unguided rockets, but this was denied by the Iranians.

At the start of Operation *Desert Storm* in August 1990 Iraqi Air Force Mi-25s, which were heavily employed during its invasion of Kuwait, were withdrawn by Saddam Hussein when it became apparent that they would be needed to help retain his grip on power in the aftermath of the Gulf War, which resulted in an Iraqi military defeat. On 7 February 1991 a USAF F-15C shot down a Mi-25 with an AIM-7M and a week later another was destroyed when it was hit by a Paveway bomb from a USAF F-15 as it took off.

Following the US-led 2003 invasion of Iraq, codenamed Operation *Iraqi Freedom*, Saddam Hussein was captured in December 2003 and the remains of his air force were destroyed.

The Iraqi Air Force was rebuilt in 2004 but as the country descended into chaos and increasing sectarian violence, by 2007 its only combat aircraft were Mi-35Ms of the 35th Attack Helicopter Squadron, based at Taji Air Base, which was deployed to support Iraqi ground troops in the fight against terrorism. A total of twenty-eight Mi-35Ms had been delivered and at least six were written off or withdrawn from use after combat damage.

Syria

The Syrian Arab Air Force (SyAAF) took delivery of more than fifty Mi-25s between 1981 and 1985 and were in action during the fifth Arab-Israeli war, which broke out in 1982. By 2000, much of the SyAAF was grounded and it was not until 2008 that the government contracted Russia's 150 Aircraft Repair Plant in Kaliningrad to overhaul thirty-six Mi-25s, but owing to Syria's failures to pay for the work, few had been returned before unrest spread throughout the country.

In June 2011 Mi-25 crews were among the first to participate in Syrian Civil War by attacking defecting army units in Idlib province and losses soon mounted. Since 2013 the SyAAF had lost at least eight to SAMs fired by rebel forces or Islamic State militants. By 2020 less than twenty Mi-25s were operational with 766 Squadron at Dmeyr and 765 Squadron at Almazza.

Libya

The Libyan Arab Air Force (LAAF) took delivery of a number of Mi-24As in the mid-1970s, followed by twenty-four Mi-25s and twelve Mi-35s in the 1980s. They were operated throughout in the Chadian Civil War, supporting pro-Libyan rebels against the French and US supported government forces. At least five were shot down by Chadian forces and another eight destroyed on the ground.

In January 1987 a LAAF Mi-25 was hit by ground fire and captured after making a forced landing in northern Chad. It was later donated by Chad to France where it underwent trials with the French military.

During the first Libyan Civil War in 2011, fought between forces loyal to Colonel Muammar Gaddafi and foreign supported groups seeking to oust his rule, more LAAF Hinds were lost to ground fire or defecting pilots. Two LAAF Mi-35s were destroyed on the ground in March 2011 by French aircraft enforcing the UN authorised no-fly zone during Operation *Unified Protector*. One Free Libyan Air Force Mi-25D that violated the no-fly-zone in April 2011 to strike loyalist positions in Ajdabiya was shot down by Libyan ground forces.

With the assistance of the UN air operations rebel forces captured and killed Gaddafi in October 2011, after which the LAAF was disbanded but re-established in 2012. By 2015 the military had split into two factions, the self-styled Libyan National Army (LNA) supported by Egypt and the United Arab Emirates (UAE) and the UN-backed Government of National Accord (GNA), and the country slid into a second civil war. Three Mi-24Ps bought by the UAE in Belarus for LNA were delivered in April 2015 and yet another bout of civil war began in 2019. An LNA Mi-35 was shot down near Misrata on 12 April 2020 by GNA forces, its three crew killed, and GNA troops captured LNA's strategic al-Watiya air base in May where six stored Mi-24As and an airworthy Mi-24P were found. In October Libya's rival forces signed a permanent ceasefire at a UN-sponsored ceasefire.

Algeria

The Algerian Air Force (AAF) has operated a mixture of thirty-wight Mi-24Ds and Mi-24Vs, the first of which were delivered 1980.

An AAF Hind was one of three Mi-24s modernised to become SuperHind Mk III by the South African company Advanced Technologies and Engineering (ATE) in 1998. The gun armament was replaced by a hydraulically driven Vektor F2 chain turret with a 20 mm GIAT cannon with external ammunition storage and its anti-tank capability improved with the long-range laser-guided ZT-3 Ingwe ATGM. ATE installed a new Doppler radar, GPS-assisted navigational system, the ARINC Mil-Std 1553 data-bus, and the Carl Zeiss Optronics Argos 410-Z airborne observation system turret.

The AAF operated twenty-four Mi-24 Mk III SuperHinds from Biskra Air Base with the 1e Regiment d'Hélicoptère de Combat, which deployed its helicopters to Forward Operating Bases (FOB) to perform counter insurgency operations on the country's south-western and eastern borders. One SuperHind crashed near Zarzaitine Airport on 9 March 2014 and another near Guemar Airport on 2 May 2019.

In 2015, Algeria ordered forty-two Mi-28NE Night Hunter combat helicopters to begin replacing the SuperHinds in 2022.

An Iraqi Air Force Mi-25 in an early pre-*Desert Storm* camouflage hangar.

An Iraqi Air Force Mi-25 assault helicopter abandoned during Operation *Desert Storm* in March 1991. (DoD)

A captured Iraqi Mi-25 at an XVIII Airborne Corps airfield during Operation *Desert Storm* prior to being transported to the United States. (DoD)

An Iraqi Mi-25 abandoned during Operation *Desert Storm* armed with UV-32-57 rocket pods, each containing thirty-two S-5 57mm rockets, and an AT-2 Swatter anti-tank missile. (DoD)

An Iraqi Army Aviation Mi-35M of the 35 Attack Helicopter Squadron equipped with engine exhaust diffusers was delivered in May 2015.

A Syrian Arab Air Force Mi-25 armed with an SPCV 12.7 mm machine gun pod. (SyAAF)

One of several Syrian Arab Air Force Mi-25s damaged at Taftanaz Asir Base in 2013 by Islamic State militants.

One of Syrian Arab Air Force Mi-25s lost to SAMs fired by rebel forces in 2013. (SyAAF)

Libyan Arab Air Force Mi-25 '854'.

Former Algerian Mi-24V was modernised by South Africa's Advanced Technologies and Engineering (ATE) in 1999 to develop the SuperHind Mk III. (David Oliver)

One of the Algerian Air Force's SuperHind Mk III, a Mi-24V modernised by ATE and Aviakon in Ukraine. (AAF)

Chapter 5

African Operators

In 2021 Russia claims to have more than 250 Mil Mi-24/35 attack helicopters in service with air arms across the African continent.

Ethiopia

The Ethiopian Air Force (EAF) received Mi-24As in 1978, which were the first Hinds to be used in combat when Somalia invaded the disputed Ogaden region of Ethiopia flown by Cuban and East German aircrews, and against Eritrean separatists during the 1980s. The Mi-24As were supplemented by Mi-35s in 1987.

The People's Democratic Republic of Ethiopia was established after a military coup in 1987, prompting the defection of several EAF Mi-35 pilots to Eritrea, Somalia and Djibouti. After a thirty-year struggle the Eritreans successfully gained independence from Ethiopia in a UN-monitored referendum in April 1993. However, border limits tensions remained and in May 1998 clashes developed into full-scale war during which the EAF lost five Mi-35s. After a UN-brokered ceasefire in June 2000, EAF defections continued. An EAF Mi-35P and its three-man crew departed Dire Dawa on 19 December 2014 for a routine training flight before it descended to low level and headed for Eritrea. The pilot had joined the EAF in 2003 and served with the Ethiopian peacekeeping mission supporting UNAMID in Darfur, Sudan, in 2010.

EAF Mi-35s were again in action against the Tigray People's Liberation Front from November 2020, during which one was shot down near Guya in Tigray state on 20 April 2021, killing its three-man crew.

Sudan

Since the Republic of Sudan won independence from the UK on 1 January 1956, it has been involved in a series of civil wars.

The Sudanese Air Force (SAF) operated a number of Hinds captured from the LAAF during the 1983–1987 Chadian Civil War against Libyan-backed rebels. In 1995, it acquired six former Soviet Mi-24V/Ps, two of which were lost during operations against the Sudanese People's Liberation Army (SPLA). Twelve more were acquired in 2001 and used extensively in the disputed region of Darfur since 2004. Three Hinds were shot down by the SPLA in 2013 and the surviving Mi-24/35s were operated by 3 Helicopter Squadron, based at Jebel Aulia at the end of 2020.

Mali

The Malian Air Force has been battling Islamist insurgents for more than a decade. In 2007 two former Bulgarian Mi-24D were acquired, piloted by contracted Ukrainians, one of which was damaged during an attack on Tuareg rebels in April 2008 and the pilot killed. Four more were delivered from Bulgaria, one of which crashed near Ouro Modi killing five crew members. In September 2017 the Malian Air Force took delivery of the two of four Mi-35Ms ordered.

The former French colony of Burkina Faso has had a long-standing border dispute with neighbouring Mali and Jihadist attacks, which escalated dramatically in 2019 despite significant military support from France. Two former Russian Mi-24s were acquired in 2005, one of which was a Mi-24V converted from a Mi-24K Hind-G2 artillery observation helicopter. In 2017 they were part of Burkina Faso's military contribution to the G5 Sahel Joint Force set up with Mali, Mauritania, Niger and Chad to fight growing Jihadist terrorist threats in the region.

Niger's air force operates two Mi-24Ps based in Niamey as part of the Multinational Joint Task Force (MNJTF) mandated to defeat Boko Haram in the region. Chad's air force acquired two Mi-24Vs from Ukraine in 2001 and another four in 2007, one of which was shot down near Abeche in June 2008. Operations against Boko Haram incursions from Nigeria began in 2015 and by 2020 the Chadian Air Force had five Mi-24Vs on strength, but few were airworthy.

Senegal

The Senegalese Air Force has three former Slovak Mi-24Vs that underwent refurbishment by Poland's WZL-1 overhaul facility at Lodz in 2017, and two Mi-35Ps equipped with the Controp DSP-HD EO/IR system. Two Mi-24Vs were deployed to the United Nations Multidimensional Integrated Stabilization Mission in the Central African Republic (MINUSCA) in 2017 at Bangui Airport, one of which crashed during an operation against Islamic rebel forces on 27 September 2019, killing four crew members.

Sierre Leone

Three Mi-24Vs owned by Sierra Leone and flown by South African military contractors were used against Revolutionary United Front (RUF) rebels in 1995, driving them from the capital, Freetown. In September 2000, they flew a Mi-24V in support of the UK's Operation *Barras*, a SAS rescue mission of British soldiers captured in Sierra Leone by the West Side Boys. Guinea also used its two Mi-25s against the RUF and provided air support to the Liberians United for Reconciliation and Democracy (LURD) insurgency in northern Liberia between 2001 and 2003.

Ivory Coast

Four Mi-24Vs from Belarus and Bulgaria were delivered to the Ivory Coast Air Force in 2002, two of which were destroyed by French troops at Yamoussoukro Airport in November 2004. The remaining Hinds were operated by the Mama Squadron at Abidjan, but on 27 November 2019 one was written off in a ground collision with a Mi-17 at Katiola and on 18 March 2020 the other Mi-24D crashed at Felix Houphouet Boigny Airport in Abidjan. Two refurbished ex-Bulgaria Mi-24Ds were delivered in August 2020.

Nigeria

The Nigerian Air Force (NAF) had a fleet of two Mi-24Ps, three Mi-35Ps and four Mi-24Vs operated by the 115th Special Operations Group at Port Harcourt and operate against Boko Haram terrorists. In 2016 the NAF began taking delivery of twenty-four Mi-35Ms, one of which crashed while providing CAS to troops in January 2019. By January 2021 the NAF had five Mi-35Ms plus two reactivated Mi-35Ps, with another eighteen Mi-35s to be delivered.

Democratic Republic of Congo

Since independence from Belgium in 1960, the Congo has been plagued by civil wars and internal military conflict. In 1996 France financed the acquisition of five Mi-24s and contracted a number of Serbian pilots and technicians. Two were never assembled while the others were plagued by technical problems. A Mi-24V hit a power line and crashed in March 1997, killing the crew of three plus four passengers. Two Mi-24Vs based at Goma and flown by Georgian and Belarus aircrews were shot down in North Kivu by militants in January 2017. The Air Force of the Democratic Republic of Congo has eight Mi-24 on its inventory.

Angola

The National Air Force of Angola's Mi-25s were initially flown by Cuban and East German crews against UNITA rebels supported by South Africa. After the foreign pilots left in 1989, few of the Hinds remained airworthy.

More than thirty Mi-24Ps were acquired between 1995 and 2016 from various sources, giving it one of the largest Hind fleets in Africa. They are operated by two squadrons of the 22nd Combat Helicopter Regiment at Huambo Air Base.

The Central African Republic received two Mi-24V/Mi-35 helicopters from the Ukraine in 2011, one of which was overhauled in Russia in May 2021.

Zimbabwe

When the Air Force of Zimbabwe (AFZ) was born out of the Royal Rhodesian Air Force in 1980, it was a well equipped professional air arm. Six Mi-35Ps were delivered in 1998 and the aircrews of No. 8 Squadron were trained at Thornhill Air Base by Russian instructors. During the Second Congo War, which lasted from August 1998 to July 2003, the AFZ attacked rebel and Rwandan offensives with its Mi-35Ps operated by No. 7 Squadron at Manyame but many are currently unserviceable due to a shortage of spares.

Uganda

The Ugandan Air Force ordered four former Belarus Mi-24s via British Virgin Islands registered company Consolidated Sales Corporation (CSC) in 1997. Two arrived in 1998 but found that they were not refurbished and were incapable of flying. Following the delivery of six Mi-24Ps from Russia, one was destroyed in an accident at Osubi Airstrip in April 2001.

On 12 August 2012 three Mi-24s departed Soroti on 12 August 2012 en route to add strength to the AU force AMISOM in Somalia. All three crashed on Mount Kenya resulting in the deaths of seven crew members while another fifteen survived. Yet another was shot down while operating in South Sudan in December 2013.

Mozambique

South African company Paramount received a contract from the Mozambique government in 2020 to supply an unspecified number of Mi-24s and train their pilots.

Left: Ukraine Army Aviation Mi-24P assigned to the United Nations Mission in Liberia (UNMIL) at Monrovia patrolling over Liberia in search of illegal marijuana plantations in 2008. (UN)

Below: One of five Ethiopian Air Force Mi-35P helicopters arrived in Nyala in Sudan to support the African Union-United Nations Mission in Darfur (UNAMID) in 2011. (UN)

Mi-24V '928' helicopter operated by the Sudanese Air Force's 3 Helicopter Squadron based at Jebel Aulia in 2007.

Four new Mi-35Ms have been delivered to the Malian Air Force.

Niger Air Force operated two Mi-24P helicopters based at Niamey in Diffa in 2016.

The Senegalese Air Force has three former Slovak Mi-24Vs refurbished by Poland's WZL-1 overhaul facility at Lodz in 2017.

A refurbished Senegalese Air Force Mi-24V at the WZL-1 facility at Lodz in Poland.

A Senegal Mi-24V deployed to the UN Multidimensional Integrated Stabilization Mission in the Central African Republic (MINUSCA) in 2017 at Bangui Airport. (UN)

Two refurbished ex-Bulgaria Mi-24Ds were delivered to the Ivory Coast Air Force in August 2020.

The Nigerian Air Force Mi-24V '529' operated by the 115th Special Operations Group at Port Harcourt in its air assault role. (Kenneth Iwelnmo)

A total of twenty-four new-build Mi-35Ms on order for the Nigerian Air Force are being delivered.

Ukraine Army Aviation Mi-24P deployed to Goma in support of the United Nations Organization Stabilization Mission in the Democratic Republic of Congo (MONUSCO) in 2015. (UN)

An Air Force of the Democratic Republic of Congo Mi-24V armed with 240mm S-24 unguided rockets. (Guido Potters)

Six Mi-35Ps were delivered to the Air Force of Zimbabwe in 1998. These are operated by No. 7 Squadron at Manyame.

Chapter 6

Asia Pacific Operators

Afghanistan

Deliveries of Mi-24As and Mi-25s to the Afghan Republican Air Force began in 1979, which were soon in action against Mujahedin guerrillas supported by Soviet Hinds (see Chapter 2).

Following the withdrawal of Soviet forces in 1989, Afghanistan imploded into a civil war between the ruling Taliban forces and various warlords, during which Mi-35s were operated by General Dostum's private army. The Hinds were regularly deployed against the resurgent Taliban until they were overthrown when US-led forces invaded Afghanistan in October 2001.

The Afghan Air Force (AAF) was reformed in January 2008 and among its first equipment were Mi-24Vs donated by Czechoslovakia followed by three Mi-35s and five former-Belarus Mi-24Vs donated by India between 2015 and 2019. Since then they have been in action against Taliban that has waged an insurgency against the US-backed Afghan governments. In 2020, US UH-60A Black Hawks, the MD 530F light attack helicopters, began replacing the Hinds, but most of these were rendered unserviceable following the US withdrawal in 2021 and the Taliban takeover.

India

In 1983, No. 125 Helicopter Squadron was formed at Pathankot Air Force Base as the Indian Air Force's first attack helicopter unit equipped with the Mi-25. The 'Gladiators' saw action as part of UN peacekeeping missions in Africa and a number of overseas operations.

During the 1987 dispute with Pakistan over sovereignty of the Siachin Glacier, the world's highest battlefield, Indian Air Force (IAF) Hinds attacked Pakistani Army positions and in the same year they supported the Indian Peace Keeping

Force (IPKF) in Sri Lanka. In Operation *Pawan* the Mi-25s were used to attack Tamil Tiger encampments, clandestine riverine traffic and escort troop-carrying helicopters.

Twenty-two Mi-35Es were delivered to No. 104 Helicopter Squadron 'Firebirds' in 1989 and in May 1999, they provided CAS to the Indian Army during the ongoing conflict with Pakistan over Kashmir during Operation *White Sea*. One was lost in an accident in Himachal Pradesh in February 2002.

The IAF Mi-35 fleet underwent a US $20 million upgrade in 2000 with the Israel Aerospace Industries Tamam Mission 24 Upgrade Package, which utilises the Helicopter Multi-mission Optronic Stabilised Payload (HMOSP) system with day-night sight with TV, FLIR and automatic target tracker integrated with helmet sight, NVG-compatible cockpit with MFDs and digital moving-map display, a new mission planning system and integrated defensive aid suite, and support for the AT-6 Spiral and Rafael Spike anti-tank missiles. One of the upgraded helicopters was lost in an accident in Himachal Pradesh in February 2002.

The IAF Hinds are being replaced by twenty-two Boeing AH-64E(I) Apaches, the first of which entered service with No. 125 Helicopter Squadron in September 2019.

Sri Lanka

In 1985 three Mi-24Vs were leased from Ukraine, which were followed by fifteen Mi-24Vs and sixteen Mi-24Ps assigned to 9 Helicopter Squadron at SLAF Minnerlya-Hingarukgoda. They were soon in action against Tamil separatists in the ongoing civil war, one of which was shot down by the Liberation Tigers of Tamil Eelam (LTTE) over the Bay of Bengal, killing eight on board, in March 1997 and another in November. Six more were lost to LTTE SAMs in the next two years. By 2001, sixteen Mi-35Ps had been added to the fleet, one of which was destroyed in a pre-dawn attack by the LTTE on SLAF Katunayake in July 2001.

At the end on 2020, 9 Helicopter Squadron operated nine M-35Ps from SLAF Hingurakgoda tasked with CAS, battlefield air interdiction, maritime air operations, armed escort missions and air defence operations.

Pakistan

In June 2017 Pakistan sent Russia a draft contract for the delivery of four Mi-35M helicopters. They were delivered to the Pakistan Army Aviation Corps under the US $153 million contract in April 2018.

North Korea

The Korean People's Army Air and Anti-Air Force (KPAAF) was established in 1948 incorporating much of the original Soviet air tactics. The KPAAF introduced the Hind into service in the 1990s and it has been reported that its 63rd Air Regiment is equipped with Mi-24Ds based at Ayang-ni near the Demilitarized Zone (DMZ), while others are operated by two regiments based at Samjangkol, which are the only dedicated assault helicopters in the KPAF's inventory.

Vietnam

The Vietnam People's Air Force (VPAF) is the successor of the former North Vietnamese Air Force and absorbed the Republic of Vietnam Air Force following the country's reunification in 1975. From the mid-1980s the VPAF used Mi-24As against Khmer Rouge guerrillas based in neighbouring Kampuchea now Cambodia.

From 1990 VPAF Mi-24Ds were operated by the 916th Helicopter Regiment at Hòa Lòc Air Base West of Hanoi, although it was not clear if they remained operational in 2020.

Australia

Australia took possession of two Mi-24R Hinds in March 1997, which had been bought in Belarus from AVIAVip KO based in Vilnius, Lithuania, by the UK-based military company Sandline International to be delivered to Papua New Guinea under a US $34 million deal for operations by Executive Outcomes against insurgents on the Isle of Bougainville in 1998. However, the An-124 that was transporting the Hinds en route from the Seychelles was intercepted by RAAF F/A-18s between Papua New Guinea and northern Australia in March 1997 and diverted to RAAF Tindal where all the arms it carried including the two Mi-24Rs were impounded. A proposed sale to Nepal fell through in 2002 and the Hinds were offered to the Darwin Aviation Museum in 2011. However, after a decade in open storage they were unfit for public display and subsequently scrapped.

Myanmar

Russia supplied Myanmar with ten Mi-24P and Mi-35Ps, which have been used against the Kachin Independence Army (KIA) since 2007. A Mi-35P was shot down by KIA Army south of Myitkyina in January 2013. The Myanmar Air Force's

Mi-35Ps were upgraded with TV/FLIR of the Russian GOES-342 family the Urals Optical system, or the Israeli Controp DSP-HD in 2016. Russian Helicopters also won a contract in 2016 to overhaul four Mi-24Ps by the 419 Aircraft Repair Plant in St Petersburg. The remaining three were worked on in-country under a partnership agreement between the Russian Helicopters and the Myanmar Air Force.

Indonesia

The first Mi-35Ps were supplied to Indonesia in September 2003 and in September 2007 and three additional Mi-35Ps were supplied in September 2010. An official ceremony to mark the handover of the helicopters to the Indonesian Army Aviation was held in October 2010, at Pondok Cabe Airport in Jakarta.

Russia's 150 Aircraft Repair Plant accepted two Indonesian Mi-35Ps as part of a contract for major repairs of the helicopters was signed in September 2016. Indonesia has a total of eight Mi-35Ps in service with the 31st Squadron of Indonesian Army Aviation, stationed at Ahmad Yani airport in Semarang.

Two MI-35 attack helicopters from the Afghan National Army Air Corps launch from the airport in Kabul, Afghanistan, on a gunnery training mission in May 2009. (DOD)

A former Czech Air Force Mi-24V that was donated to Afghanistan in 2007 and struck off charge in 2016. (USAF)

Afghan National Army Air Corps Mi-35s deployed to a remote mountain location during national elections in 2011. (USAF)

Another former Czech Mi-24V donated to the Afghan National Army Air Corps patrolling the mountains range surrounding Kabul in 2012. (USAF)

An Indian Air Force Mi-25 belonging to No. 125 Helicopter Squadron finished in its original semi-gloss camouflage scheme. (A. A. Singh)

Armed with UV-32-57 rocket launchers, Indian Air Force Mi-25s were deployed to Sri Lanka to support the Indian Peace Keeping Force in 1987. (A. A. Singh)

An Indian Air Force Mi-25 wearing a revised camouflage scheme and armed with UB-32A-24 pods with 80 mm S-8 unguided rockets. (IAF)

Indian Air Force Mi-35E Z3134 was part of the Indian Aviation Contingent II to the UN Organization Mission in the Democratic Republic of the Congo MONUC at Goma in 2008. (IAF)

One of the Indian Air Force's Mi-35s upgraded in 2000 with the Israel Aerospace Industries Tamam Mission 24 Upgrade Package.

Sri Lanka Air Force Mi-35P SAH4407 operated by 9 Helicopter Squadon at Minneriya-Hingarukgoda. (Rehman Abubakr)

A small number of Mi-24As were exported to Vietnam in the 1980s, which were replaced by Mi-24Ds from 1990. (M. Radizi Desa)

A US Army AH-64E Apache and an Indonesian Army Aviation Mi-35P take off together during *Garuda Shield* 2014. (US Army)

CHAPTER 7

Latin American Operators

Cuba

The Cuban Revolutionary Air and Air Defense Force (CRA/ADF) was established after the Cuban Revolution in 1958. Twelve Mi-25s were delivered in 1981 flown by East German pilots. With the support of the Soviet Union, in 1990 the CRA/ADF was one of the best equipped in Latin America but when its support was withdrawn over the next decade, it went into decline. By 2020 the 3684 Helicopter Regiment based at Cienfuegos Air Base operated three Mi-25s and a single Mi-35 delivered in 2008, while another seven Hinds were in storage.

Nicaragua

From 1981, the United States began efforts to overthrow the left-wing Sandinista Revolutionary Government of Nicaragua. This included CIA support of right-wing guerilllas based in neighbouring Honduras and Costa Rica known as Contras. The Sandinista Revolutionary Air Force acquired a total of twenty-two Mi-25s in 1984, which the US Administration regarded as a major escalation of tensions in Central America.

During December 1984 the Mi-25s were in action against the Contras in Jinotega Province, near the border of Honduras, but in 1987 FIM-43 Redeye man-portable air-defence systems (MANPADS) were suppled to the Contras. Seven Mi-25s were shot down by the MANPADS during 1987 while another was damaged near the Honduran border, when it was intercepted by Honduran F-86 Sabres. Another was flown to Honduras by a defecting Sandinista pilot in December 1988.

In February 1989 a peace accord was agreed by Nicaragua and the neighbouring states and the Contras were disbanded. Most of the Hinds were sold to Peru in 1992, although the Nicaraguan Air Force operated fleet of twelve Mi-24s and Mi-25s until 2017.

Peru

The Peruvian Air Force took delivery of twelve Mi-24Ds and two Mi-24DUs in 1983 initially operated by the Special Forces Group based at Victor Air Base in southern Peru. They were followed by four Nicaraguan Mi-24Ds and three Mi-25Ds. Another twelve new aircraft were delivered to Grupo Aéreo No. 3 in 1985 together with a PTV-241 Flight Simulator, based at Callao Air Base near Lima. In June 1989 they were deployed against Shining Path Maoist guerrillas in Peruvian highlands .

The Mi-25s were later operated by Grupo Aéreo No. 2 at Base Aérea de Vitor and deployed to Huallaga in January 1995 during the Cenepa War. One was written off on 7 February 1995 during an attack on Ecuadorian troops in the area of Base Sur when it was shot down by Ecuadorian forces with a 9K38 Igla MANPADS. Two Mi-25s were lost in a mid-air collision near Vitor in August 1995.

After withdrawal from service in 2001 due to maintenance problems, some were returned to service in early 2008 following a limited local overhaul. In April 2011 two new-build Mi-35Ps were delivered and the Peruvian Government signed a US $20 million contract with the Russian arms export agency Rosoboronexport for Stage 1 life extension refurbishment of six Mi-25/35s at Aircraft Repair Plant 810 at Chita in Siberia to extend the life of the helicopters by thirty years or 4,000 hours.

Air Squadron 211, 'Dragons of the Air' of Grupo Aéreo No. 2, operated a mixed fleet of sixteen Mi-24Ds and Mi-35Ps in 2020 undertaking anti-drug missions in the valley of the Apurímac, Ene and Mantaro rivers (VRAEM) region.

Venezuela

Venezuela was the first Latin American customer for the Mi-35M. The first of ten Mi-35M Caribe helicopters were delivered to the Venezuelan Army Air Service in July 2006 and accepted into service at Base Aerea 'El Libertador' at Maracay in November 2006. Venezuela received the first upgraded Mi-35M2 helicopters from a total of ten that were upgraded in Russia by Rostvertol at the beginning of 2017. One was written off when it crashed near El Pao in February 2019 during a training flight after experiencing technical problems, injuring five on board. Despite US imposed sanctions, the Venezuelan Army Air Service remains well funded.

Brazil

In December 2006 Brazil signed a US $326 million contract with the Russian arms export agency Rosoboronexport for twelve Mi-35M4 helicopters, designated in Brazilian Air Force service as the AH-2 Sabre. Delivery was delayed while the helicopters were fitted with Elbit Systems' avionics by Elbit's Brazilian subsidiary

AEL to enable them to operate in a forest region with high temperatures and humidity, and fly continuous day-night missions.

Operated by the 2nd 'Poti' Squadron in the 8th Aviation Group based at Porto Velho in Rondonia state, the AH-2 Sabres were used in the Amazon region near Bolivia's northern border. During Operation *Ostium*, launched in March 2017, tasked with countering illicit flights along the borders with Paraguay and Bolivia carrying arms and narcotics to Brazil, the AH-2s operated in conjunction with Brazil Air Force Embraer E-99 AEW&Cs and A-29B Super Tucanos.

However, the type had not been popular with Air Force officers, suffering from serviceability and quality issues. In 2020 it was reported that the AH-2 Sabres had been offered for sale to the Libyan National Army (LNA) financed by the United Arab Emirates, but they were never delivered. In April 2021 Russian Helicopters announced that it had signed a contract the Brazilian company IAS to tackle some technical issues to enable the AH-2s to resume operations. In 2023 the AH-2s were for sale.

Peruvian Air Force Mi-25 '694' based at Grupo Aéreo No. 2 at Base Aérea de Vitor was modernised by Russia's Aircraft Repair Plant 810 in 2011. (FAP)

Peruvian Air Force Mi-25 '695' took part in an attack on Ecuadorian troops in February 1995 and was written-off in August 1995 in a mid-air collision with another Mi-25. (FAP)

A Venezuelan Air Force Mi-35M Caribe firing unguided rockets during a training exercise. (FAV)

One of Venezuelan Air Force Caribes upgraded to Mi-35M2 standard by Rostvertal in 2017. (Rostvertol)

Designated in Brazilian Air Force service as the AH-2 Sabre, twelve Mi-35M4s are operated by the 2nd 'Poti' Squadron in the 8th Aviation Group at Porto Velho. (Joao Paulo Moralez)

The Brazilian Air Force AH-2 Sabres are operated in the Amazon region near Bolivia's northern border. (FAB)

During Operation *Ostium* in March 2017, Brazilian Air Force AH-2 Sabres were tasked with countering illicit flights along the borders with Paraguay and Bolivia. (FAB)

The last of twelve Mi-35M4s to be delivered to the Brazilian Air Force at Rostvertol. (David Oliver)

Chapter 8

Post-Cold War Conflicts

Croatia

The Croatian Air Force was established in December 1991, during the Croatian War of Independence from the Yugoslav federation. Croatia obtained two Mi-24Ds and two Mi-24Vs, one of which was lost in June 1995 during the Yugoslav civil war. One of the Mi-24Ds was converted to the search and rescue role. Their service life expired in 2000, and the 29th Combat Helicopter Squadron based at Zagreb-Pleso that operated them was disbanded in 2005.

Nagorno-Karabakh

The Nagorno-Karabakh War was an ethnic and territorial conflict between former Soviet republics Azerbaijan and Armenia from the late 1980s to May 1994. Mi-24s on both sides took an active part in the conflict and in February 1992 an Azerbaijan Air Force (AzAF) Mi-24V was written off on a low-level training flight when crashed into lake Masazyrgol. Another was hit by small-arms fire in April while providing CAS to Azerbaijani troops in the Füzuli/Varanda district. The following month another Mi-24 was hit by a MANPADS and crashed while attacking Armenian positions in Agdam district.

In June, two Armenian Mi-24Ps were hit by Azerbaijan ground fire and crash-landed in Nagorno-Karabakh, their crews escaping capture. Between the end of 1992 and January 1994 the AzAF had lost five Mi-24Vs. In May 1994, with a Russia-brokered agreement, both sides agreed to end hostilities, by which time the AzAF had lost nine Mi-24s and had only six left in its inventory. The Armenian Air Force lost four Hinds.

In late September 2020 fighting broke out along the border between Azerbaijan, supported by Turkey and Russia, and Armenia, the most serious escalation of the unresolved conflict since 2016 when an AzAF Mi-24V was shot down by Artsakh Republic forces. In the 2020 conflict AzAF Mi-24s saw limited use and none were shot down. However, a Russian Air Force Mi-24P was accidentally shot down on 9 November 2020 at Yeraskh in the Arabat province of Armenia by an Azerbaijan MANPADS. On 10 November another Russia-brokered ceasefire agreement ended six weeks of warfare over the disputed territory.

Chechnya

On 15 December 1994 Russian invaded the breakaway Caucasian republic of Chechnya after negotiations failed between President Yelsin and Dudayev. By late March 1995, Russia had deployed fifty-two Mi-24s, three of which were lost to hostile fire in the first three months of the conflict.

Armed conflict between Russian forces and Chechnya separatists and the border regions of North Caucasus broke out again in August 1999. Russian Hinds undertook CAS and reconnaissance missions during the combat phase of the Second Chechen War that lasted until 2003. The Russian Air Force lost a total of nineteen Mi-24P/Vs, many of them shot down by Strela MANPADS.

Macedonia

Macedonia was the only one of the former Yugoslav republics to gain its independence through peaceful means but was subject to a 1991 UN arms embargo when the Yugoslav civil war broke out. When a crisis between ethnic Albanian insurgents and Macedonian government forces broke out in March 2001, the Macedonian Air Warfare and Air Defence Forces had no helicopters until Ukraine donated eight Mi-24Vs. The first Hind combat operation was against Albanian Separatists near Tetovo on 2 April with 57 mm rockets and Shturm-V anti-tank missiles. During a night attack on the village of Aracinovo, Mi-24s dropped 250-kg bombs. The Mi-24s, flown by foreign pilots, proved to be the most important air asset in combat and none were lost when conflict ended with the Ohrid Agreement in August 2001. In December 2001, Macedonia received two Mi-24K photo-reconnaissance and artillery spotting Hinds from Ukraine, all of which were assigned to the 201st Anti-armour Helicopter Squadron.

Georgia

The Georgian Air Force and Air Defense Division was established in January 1992 and the first combat flights were conducted in September during the separatist war in Abkhazia, during which one of its Mi-24Vs was shot down near Gagra by an Igla MANPADS on 5 October. An armed conflict between Russia and Georgia broke out in the territory of Georgia's breakaway regions of South Ossetia and Abkhazia in August 2008.

Georgia's small force of Mi-24Ps based at Alexeevka-Tblisi played no role in the war after the first day, although at least two were destroyed on the ground at Senaki Air Base. The military campaign lasted only five days until the parties reached a preliminary ceasefire agreement mediated by the European Union.

Russian air incursions into Georgia had been ongoing for over a year prior to the outbreak of war. In March 2007, Russian Mi-24 helicopters attacked Georgian government buildings in the Kodori Gorge, the only portion of Abkhazia then under Georgian government control.

After the war, the Georgian Air Force and Air Defence Division was abolished until the Georgian government decided to re-establish the air force as its own separate arm in 2016 with plans to get rid of almost its entire Soviet helicopter inventory and replace it with Western aircraft.

Ukraine

Established in 1992 after the collapse of the Soviet Union, the Ukrainian Army Aviation force inherited a large number of Mi-24P and Mi-24V helicopters. For the next two decades, the armed forces were underfunded and its equipment became difficult to maintain. In Africa, Ukrainian Mi-24Ps served with the United Nations Mission in Liberia (UNMIL) and the United Nations Organization Stabilization Mission in the DR Congo (MONUSCO) in 2012.

Russia's annexation of Crimea in 2014 prompted a potential civil war in Ukraine with militias formed by the predominantly Russian-speaking populations of Donetsk, Slavyansk and Kramatorsk, cities in south-eastern and eastern Ukraine on the borders with Russia. Ukrainian armed forces moved into the region to quell the uprisings supported by Army Aviation Mi-24s.

During a major escalation of the conflict in May 2014, two Mi-24P Hinds were shot down by Russian MANPADS in the Donetsk region, killing five crew. A third was shot down by ground fire on 5 May while on an anti-terrorist mission over Slavyansk, although the crew were uninjured and the helicopter was retrieved by Ukrainian ground forces. On 4 June a Mi-24V was hit by a MANPADS and made a forced landing injuring both crew.

The Ukrainian Army Aviation's priority was now to equip its Mi-24s with modern defensive aid suites (DAS) as these helicopters are highly vulnerable to MANPADS due to flying at low levels and comparatively low speeds. As part of a US $166,000 Ukroboronprom contract, in 2017 Aviakon modernised a number of Mi-24s. The PU-1 upgrade incorporated state-of-the-art mission systems such as the LKK-V guided missile control system produced by the Izium Instrument & Apparatus Factory, the TsKB ASP-17VPM-V enhanced-capability sighting system and improved communications. Packaged into the PU-2 upgrade was a Sagem OLSP-410L1 multi-payload optronic turret and THL-5NV hard helmet with PNL-3 night vision goggles (NVG) developed by the Polish company PCO S.A. The upgraded Mi-24Ps were also equipped with KUV 26-50 chaff/flare launchers and an Adros KT-01AVE active IR jammer.

It was not until July 2020 that an EU-brokered ceasefire came into force, but on 24 February 2022, Russia invaded Ukraine. At the time, the Ukraine Army Aviation's fleet of active Mi-24s was only thirty-five helicopters and in the first few weeks of the conflict, more than ten were lost in the fighting, although Russia lost a high number of Mi-24Ps and Mi-35Ms (see Chapter 12). On 1 April, two Ukraine Mi-24s took part in a daring low-level dawn raid on a fuel depot in the Russian city of Belograd, located some 25 miles from the border of Ukraine.

More than fifty Russian Air Force Mi-24s, wearing white identification bands, were used against separatists during the five-year Second Chechan War. (Russian MoD)

The Georgian Air Force and Air Defence Division's Mi-24V '05' was destroyed on the ground at Senaki in August 2008 by a Russian air raid. (Marcus Fülber)

The Ukrainian Army Aviation inherited Mi-24V '04 Yellow' from Russia after the collapse of the Soviet Union in 1992. (Ukraine MOD)

Mi-24V with white identification stripes during the conflict with Russian separatist militia in 2014.

Ukrainian Mi-24V '15 Blue' was one of two shot down by MANPADS on 20 August 2014. (Ukraine MOD)

A Ukraine Army Aviation Mi-24V refurbished by the state-owned Aviakon repair plant at Konotop in 2007. (Ukraine MOD)

One of the Mi-24PU2 development aircraft equipped with a Sagem OLSP-410L1 multi-payload optronic turret. (Ukraine MOD)

CHAPTER 9

US Hind War Games

When the Soviets deployed the Mi-24 to Eastern Europe and later Afghanistan, it posed a real threat to NATO and the United States in particular. The US Army's National Training Center (NTC) at Fort Irwin in California was responsible for training Blue Forces to fight realistic Opposing Forces (OPFOR) equipped with real Soviet equipment, but in the late 1980s no Mi-24s were available and it had to make do with four modified Bell UH-1H Hueys to simulate them with a fibreglass Hind nose, M22 anti-tank missile racks and the MILES laser training system.

These were followed by Sikorsky S-55s converted by Orlando Helicopter Airways with fibreglass Mi-24-type cockpits, a five-bladed main rotor, an infra-red emitter and chaff dispensers. They were designed to be flown as unmanned targets with a Honeywell remote control system and used by the US Army for Stinger MANPADS testing at the White Sands missile range in New Mexico.

When a serviceable Libyan Arab Air Force Mi-25 was found abandoned at Wadi Doum in northern Chad it was captured by Chadian forces in March 1987 and offered to the United States. The Hind was subsequently flown to N'Djamena slung under an MH-47 Chinook of the 160th Special Operations Aviation Group of US Army Aviation and then transported to the United States by a USAF C-5A as part of a clandestine CIA operation codenamed *Mountain Hope III* in June 1988.

The Mi-25 was refurbished and equipped with the ATGM tubes of the Mi-24V and was operated by the US Army Operational Test and Evaluation Command's Threat Support Activity (OTSA) at Fort Bliss in Texas until 2006. It was followed by a former-East German Mi-24D in 1991 and was operated by the US Army Threat Systems Management Office (TSMO) named 'Patience' from Biggs Army Airfield at Fort Bliss. A Mi-25 captured from Iraq during Gulf War in 1991 was evaluated by the US Air Force at Tonapah Test Range Airport and took part in All Service Combat Identification Evaluation Test (ASCIENT) training, which was conducted at the US Army Training Support center, Fort Stewart, Georgia, in 1995. After the CAS phase of training, the ground battle started with former Soviet T-72 tanks and BMP armored vehicles, supported by the Mi-25, which was later operated by the TSMO before being stored at Fort Eustis in Virginia.

In 2003 five former Bulgarian Mi-24Ds were acquired by Vertol Systems Co. Inc., allegedly a front company of the CIA, and were offered to be contracted by United States Special Operations Command (USSOCOM), but rejected because of lack of current certificate of airworthiness. Two more Bulgarian Mi-24Ds were registered to Mi-24 #120 LLC of Irving, Texas, in 2006, which made them available for adversary orientation training for the US military through a partnership with Tacoma, Washington-based VTS Aviation LLC (VTSA), and System Studies & Simulation (S3) Inc. out of Huntsville, Alabama. The training continues a legacy that started during the Cold War, when the US Army operated Hinds as part of a classified exploitation programme.

The VTS's Hinds have become a regular site at US military bases as the Pentagon demands increasingly realistic high-end training. The US Marine Air Ground Task Force Training Command filed a solicitation in April 2018, requesting a Mi-24 Hind attack helicopter capable of using AN/ASQ-T50(V)2 tracking pods compatible with the training range in Yuma, Arizona. The attack helicopter, due to its size, flight profile, firepower and defensive maneuvering capabilities, would constitute a unique threat creating a realistic, dissimilar and credible opposing force, the solicitation read. The attack helicopter was intended to be used to interrupt Marines calling in close air support (CAS) and conducting artillery and air defense missions. Additionally, the solicitation requested an aircraft capable of conducting 'intelligence collection on friendly forces' and 'air-to-ground attack of friendly forces.'

In training exercises, the helicopter would act as the aggressor force, pitted against Marine fixed-wing and rotary-wing aircraft, as well as forward operating bases, forward refueling points and anti-aircraft artillery units.

In November 2019 a US Air Force rescue-helicopter squadron flew mock battles against the two VTS Mi-24s. The war game over Davis-Monthan Air Force Base in Arizona helped prepare the base's resident 55th Rescue Squadron for intensive warfare that could involved helicopter-on-helicopter combat. In the air-to-air mode, the Hind can use its nose-mounted cannon and unguided and guided rockets to attack enemy helicopters. The USAF considered that it is arguably easier for a helicopter to attack another helicopter than it is for a supersonic fighter aircraft to do so, as its high speed can make it difficult for the pilot to get a clear shot before he passes overhead.

For that reason the USAF assigns subsonic A-10 Warthogs to escort rescue helicopters and protect them from enemy helicopters, although it considers that a Hind could be an even better counter-helicopter platform.

The US Army's Opposing Forces element at Fort Irwin used four modified UH-1H Hueys in the 1980s to simulate Mi-24 Hinds. (US Army)

A Libyan Air Force Mi-25 abandoned in northern Chad was airlifted by a MH-47 Chinook of the US Army's 160th Special Operations Aviation Group to N'Djamena as part of the CIA operation *Mountain Hope III*. (DoD)

Former East German Mi-24D, '91-32472' named 'Patience' operated by OTSA at Biggs Army Airfield at Fort Biggs taking part in a live-fire exercise in 1997. (US Army)

Former East German Mi-24P '91-22270' was acquired by the US Army from the German Army in 1991. (US Army)

Mi-24P Hind-F '91-22270' at the US Army Test and Evaluation Center, Threat Support Activity, NAS Fallon, Nevada, in 2008. (USAF)

VTS Aviation's former Bulgarian Air Force Mi-24D 'N118NX' flown by US Marine Corps aircrew at Fort Yuma in 2015. (USMC)

VTS Aviation's Mi-24D 'N120NX' flies over Ryan Airfield, Arizona, in November 2019 during an exercise with the USAF's 55th Rescue Squadron. (USAF)

CHAPTER 10

NATO Hinds

Czech Republic

The Czech Air Force, together with the Slovak Air Force, succeeded the Czechoslovak Air Force in 1993. The Czech Republic became a member of NATO in 1999.

An advisory group of the Czech Air Force was sent to Afghanistan in April 2008 to assist in the establishment of the new Afghan National Army. As a part of the international Operational Mentoring and Liaison Team (OMLT) they worked as instructors training Afghan Mi-25 helicopter aircrew and ground personnel.

By 2020 the Czech Air Force operated a fleet of fifteen Mi-24V and Mi-35s with 221st Helicopter Squadron based at a Namest nad Oslavou. They are regular participants in NATO exercises and although they have had limited upgrades by LOM Praha, including an AVS-9 NVG system, they are due to be replaced by four Bell AH-1Z Viper attack helicopters and eight UH-1Y Venom utility helicopters from 2023. At least two Hinds were donated to Ukraine in 2022.

After the formal dissolution of Czechoslovakia on 1 January 1993, the Slovak Air Force was formed and redesignated the Air Force of the Armed Forces of the Slovak Republic in 2002 before becoming a member of NATO in 2004. On 20 September 2011, all of its remaining Mi-24Vs were retired.

Hungary

The Hungarian Air Force fleet of Mi-24Vs was reinforced in 1993 by fourteen second-hand Mi-24Vs and six former East German Mi-24Ps donated by the unified Germany. Only two Mi-24Ps were overhauled and re-entered service, while the remaining Hinds were placed in long-term storage. Hungary joined NATO in 1999.

In February 2010 Hungarian Air Force air and ground crews from the 86th 'Szolnok' Helicopter Base arrived at Kabul in Afghanistan to train Afghan National

Army Air Corps Mi-35 crews. The Hungarians agreed to a provisional year-long tour, with three teams of ten instructors in four-month rotations.

The Hungarian Air Force's 86th Helicopter Base operates twelve Mi-24s at Kecskemet Air Base that have undergone modernization in Russia under a €70 million contract at the 419th Aircraft Repair Plant at St Petersburg. They were equipped with integrated GPS, instrument landing system (ILS), and NVG capability and will have another seven years of service from 2019, or 2,000 flight hours.

The role of the Mi-24s will be expanded to be deployed in emergency situations to support the civilian population. They are due to be replaced by sixteen Airbus Helicopters H145Ms equipped with HForce weapons management system, the first of which was delivered in 2020.

Poland

In 1996, Poland also received eighteen former East German Mi-24Ds donated by Germany. The Polish MoD decided to overhaul and reintroduce sixteen of the ex-German Hinds into service, using the remaining two as spare parts donors before joining NATO in 1999.

At the end of 2004 Polish Army Aviation Mi-24Ds were deployed to Iraq where they served for five years. One crashed on 18 July 2006 in Al Diwaniyah while others were not returned to Poland due to their age, condition, and high shipping costs. Some were transferred to the new Iraqi Army or scrapped.

Another Polish Mi-24W contingent was deployed to Afghanistan assigned to the 438th Air Expeditionary Group, a joint team of American, Czechoslovakian and Hungarian advisors which stood up in November 2008 at Kabul Airport to train Afghanistan National Army Air Corps Mi-35 aircrew and maintenance personnel. However, between July 2009 and June 2011, five Polish Mi-24Ws operating from a military base in Ghazni province were damaged while attempting emergency landings after being hit by ground fire or suffering mechanical problems.

The Polish Army Aviation's Mi-24D/Mi-24V fleet currently numbers some twenty-nine aircraft operated by two squadron at the 56th Air Base at Inowroclaw-Latkowo and a third at the 49th Air Base at Pruszec Gdanski.

Polish defence industry proposed a comprehensive upgrade, including a new integrated avionics system with head-up and multi-function displays, the Rafael Toplite electro-optical/infrared sensor turret and new DAS equipment. In October 2020 Poland confirmed that the Mi-24 weapons system were to include NATO standard munitions, including Rafael Spike air-to-surface missiles, the Piorun air-to-air missile, new rocket launchers and 12.7 mm machine guns.

The Polish government issued a tender for the supply of new attack helicopters in 2020, with an initial batch of sixteen to be delivered by 2026. Previously known as the Kruk programme, Poland ordered a total of 96 Boeing AH-64E Apache helicopters in 2022 to replace the Hinds.

Bulgaria

In 2000 the Bulgarian Air Force's Stara Zagora air base operating Mi-24Vs was closed and many of the Hinds withdrawn from service. After becoming a member of NATO in 2004 the Bulgarian Defence Ministry signed a contract in early 2005 with Elbit Systems of Israel to upgrade its fleet of six Mi-24V Hind-Es but the contract was eventually cancelled in 2007. After being grounded in 2010, the Bulgarian defence ministry authorised the general overhaul and life extension of the fleet in 2012, and two of the Mi-24Vs were overhauled at the TEREM-Letes Aircraft Repair Plant at Sofia between 2015 and 2018. The life-cycle extension could extend their use until the end of 2024. They are operated by the 1/24 Helicopter Aviation Squadron at Krumovo Air Base. Four more Mi-24Vs, grounded since 2000, are being returned to service as no replacement has been selected.

Slovakia

The Slovak Air Force, known since 2002 as the Air Force of the Armed Forces of the Slovak Republic, had a fleet of former Czechoslovak Mi-24 based at Silac when the country joined NATO in 2004. Eight Mi-24s were withdrawn from service on 20 September 2011 and replaced by nine UH-60M Black Hawks.

North Macedonia

In March 2020, the Republic of North Macedonia became NATO's newest member. Its Air Brigade provides air support and transport for the Army units and observation of airspace of the republic. In times of natural disasters, it also performs civil search and rescue, fire fighting and medical evacuation.

Six former Ukraine Mi-24Vs are assigned to the Combat Helicopter 'Night Hunters' Squadron based at Petrovec Airport near Skopje. They have been upgraded with Elbit Systems ANVIS/HUD24T Helmet Display and Tracking System and equipped with NATO compatible communication systems. Elbit also supplied a full mission Mi-24 simulator that includes 6 degrees of freedom motion platform by Moog, and equipped with the same avionics installed on upgraded the Mi-24s.

Georgia

Georgia was granted a NATO military assistance package in 2014, which included acquiring military equipment from alliance members and partners to lift the unofficial arms ban on Georgia. It re-established its air force in 2016 as its own separate arm and it planned to get rid of almost its entire Soviet helicopter inventory and replace it with Western aircraft.

In 2020 the Georgian Air Force's Mixed Aviation Squadron operated five Mi-24Vs from Alekseyevka Military Airfield. As part of the move to update and modernise the air fleet, two more are being refurbished by Tbilisi Aircraft Manufacturing plant, which were expected to be added to the force at the end 2021.

The Czech Air Force's Mi-35 '7356' is one of the youngest NATO Hinds that was delivered in June 2003.

Seen at the UK Royal International Air Tattoo in 2016, Mi-35 '7356' is operated by the 221st Helicopter Squadron based at Namest nad Oslavou. (David Oliver)

A Czech airman of 221st Helicopter Squadron, 22nd Helicopter Squadron, performs maintenance on an Mi-24V helicopter during Exercise Allied Spirit VI at Hohenfels Training Area, Germany, in March 2017. (US Army)

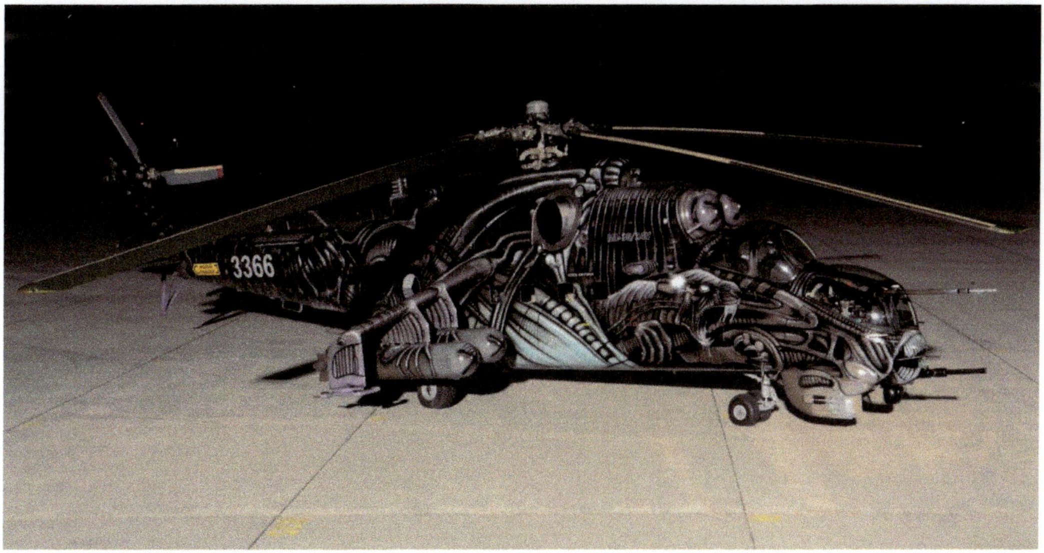

Czech Air Force Mi-35 '3366' painted in an 'Alien Tiger' colour scheme for the 2016 NATO Tiger Meet. (CzAF)

Hungarian Air Force Mi-24V '714' delivered in 1985 painted in a special 'Golden Hind' colour scheme in 2007. (József Süveg)

Flying the European Union flag, Mi-24V '720' was one of eight Hungarian Hinds overhauled by Russia's 419th ARZ at Gorelovo in 2017. (David Oliver)

A Hungarian Air Force Mi-24P launches for an orientation flight with AH-64 pilots from the 12th Combat Aviation Brigade at Szolnok Air Base, Hungary during exercise *Saber Guardian 21*. (US Army)

An elaborate eagle paint scheme worn by Hungarian Air Force Mi-24V '716' belonging to the 86th Szolnok Helicopter Base in 2010.

Hungarian Air Force Mi-24Ps of the 86th Helicopter Base and US Army AH-64 Apaches of the 12th Combat Aviation Brigade fly in formation during exercise *Saber Guardian 21*. (US Army)

Polish Army Aviation Mi-24D '457' was delivered in 1984 and based at Pruszcz Gdanski until it moved to Katowice in 2019. (PAF)

Polish Army Aviation Mi-24 V '741' wearing identity stripes prior to deploying to Iraq. (PAF)

Former East German Mi-24D '270' with eyes on the engine intake filters was one of three Polish Army Aviation Hind deployed to Iraq in 2004. (US Army)

A weather-beaten Polish Army Aviation's Mi-24Ds deployed to the Combat Aviation Brigade Iraq in 2004, most of which were scrapped in 2009. (US Army)

A Polish Mi-24W contingent was deployed to Afghanistan in 2008 and assigned to Task Force 49, operating in Ghazni Province. (Polish MoD)

A Polish Army Aviation Mi-24W involved in combat operations in Afghanistan between 2008 and 2014. (Polish MoD)

Former East German Mi-24D '270' was delivered to the Polish Army Aviation in 1996 and assigned to the 56th Air Base at Inowroclaw-Latkowo.

One of the Bulgaria Air Force's six Mi-24Vs, '142', is armed with twin 7.2 mm 9-A-622 machine gun pods. (Bulgarian MoD)

Bulgarian Air Force MI-24V '143' takes part in a live-fire exercise as part of *Shabla 19*. (DoD)

Former Czechoslovakian Mi-24V '0927' made the last flight of an Air Force of the Armed Forces of the Slovak Republic Hind in August 2011. (Miroslav Stanko)

A retired Slovak Air Force Mi-24V was used during a NATO CBRN decontamination exercise Toxic Lance in 2018. (Texas Military Department)

One of two former Soviet Mi-24K camera-equipped reconnaissance variants operated by the Macedonian Air Force. (Rob Schleiffert)

Former Ukraine Air Force Mi-24V '207' delivered to the Macedonian Air Force in 2001 and operated by the 201st Anti-tank Helicopter Squadron. (Filip Vidinovski)

Georgian Air Force aircraft including Mi-24s are being overhauled by Tbilisi Aircraft Manufacturing. (TAM)

Chapter 11

Twentieth-century Eastern Operators

Armenia

The Armenian Air Force was created in October 1992, with Mi-24s taken over from the former Soviet 7th Guards Helicopter Regiment. Having been involved in several territorial conflicts with Azerbaijan, the latest in 2020, the Armenian Air Force currently operates twelve Mi-24P/Vs assigned to the 15th Mixed Aviation Regiment, a composite helicopter squadron based at Yerevan-Erebuni.

Azerbaijan

The Azerbaijan Air Force (AzAF) was established in 1992 after the country gained its independence from the former Soviet Union. It inherited a large number of Hinds including Mi-24Rs that were later converted to Mi-24Ps. Some were involved in the two conflicts with Armenia in 1992 and 2016 (see Chapter 8).

In 2011 Azerbaijan ordered twenty-four Mi-35Ms that were delivered between 2012 and 2014, serving with 1 Squadron at Qala, which is operated by the Azerbaijan Border Guard Service.

In cooperation with the South African company ATE, the Ukrainian Aviakon Aircraft Repair Plant upgraded nine Mi-24s to SuperHind Mk IV standard, designated by the Azeri military as Mi-24Gs, 'Gele' meaning 'night'. The SuperHind Mk IV was an upgraded version of the Mk III supplied to Algeria, featuring the Pall vortex engine air particle separator system over the engine intakes.

The Mi-24Gs have been stored since 2018 while seventeen Mi-24V/Ps remain in service with 2 Squadron 'Griffins' at Qala Air Base, which can be armed with the short-range TV/IR-guided Elbit Spike-ER air-to-surface missiles.

Belarus

The Air Force and Air Defence Force of the Republic of Belarus was formed in 1992 from the 26th Air Army of the Soviet Air Forces. In 1995 Belarus had a fleet of seventy-four Mi-24s, few of which were serviceable. By 2001 the number had reduced to fifty-eight at the 181st Combat Helicopter Base in Pruzhany, which was closed in 2015. They were transferred to the 50th Composite Aviation Base at Minsk-Machulishchy. Between 1995 and 2018 Belarus sold more than fifty Mi-24s to African countries including Ethiopia, Sierra Leone, Sudan and Uganda.

In 2020 a mixed fleet of twelve Mi-24P and Mi-24Vs remain on strength including some Mi-24Ks, the Hind-G2 artillery spotting and combat reconnaissance variant. In September 2016 the Belarusian 558th Aircraft Repair Plant and the Russian's Vertolety Rossii signed a contract to overhaul some Mi-24s, while others were upgraded in Belarus by the Orsha Aircraft Repair Plant, some of which were test flown with TV3117VMA-SBM1V engines supplied by the Ukrainian company Motor Sich.

A Belarus Mi-24 crashed on approach to Pruzhany Air Base during a training flight in November 2011, killing its crew of three, while a Mi-24P was written-off in April 2016 when it crashed on landing in Gomel oblast.

In 2020, Belarus ordered an initial batch of four Mi-35M helicopters, the first of which was to be delivered at the end of 2021. The Air Force and Air Defence Force has a requirement for twelve Mi-35Ms to replace its Mi-24s.

Kazakhstan

The Kazakhstan Air Defence Force was formed in 1993 at the end of the Soviet Era. Its 486th Helicopter Regiment based at Ucharal was equipped with former Soviet Mi-24s. In July 2013 the unit's twenty Mi-24D/Vs relocated to Zhana-Semei Air Base, which had been closed for ten years.

Following a contract signed in 2017, the Kazakhstan Air Defence Force is taking delivery of ten Mi-35Ms, the first four of which were delivered in December 2016. The type is operated from the 602nd Air Base at Shymkent in western Kazakhstan as part of the country's rearmament programme.

Tajikistan

The Tazik Air and Air Defense Forces were established in 1994 and by 2006 its rotary wing capability was provided with twelve Mi-24 helicopters by Russia and operated by the Independent Helicopter Squadron at Ayni Air Force Base, although only six were airworthy in 2021.

India's defence ministry had signed a basing agreement with Tajikistan in 2002 that gives it access to Ayni Air Base, which is also shared with the Russians, who are responsible to Tazikistan's air defence. Under this trilateral agreement, the runway was extended, and the control tower renovated in 2010.

Uzbekistan

The Uzbekistan Air Force currently operates a fleet of twenty-four former Soviet Mi-24D/P/V variants operated by the 66th Separate Helicopter Regiment based at Chirchik Airbase, 30 km from Tashkent. In 2002 SAGEM was contracted to upgrade twelve Mi-24Vs with CH-2H NVGs and compatible cockpit lighting, a nose-mounted Nadir FLIR ball turret alongside a day camera and laser designator, a SAMIR missile warning system tied to existing Russian chaff/flare dispensers and a STRIX gyro-stabilised sighting system for target detection and identified compatible with HOT anti-tank missiles and Mistral AAMs. The work was carried out at workshops in Tashkent.

An Uzbec Mi-24 crashed at Chirchik Air Base in July 2009, killing two of the crew. In 2018 the Uzbekistan ordered twelve new Mi-35M helicopters to replace the Mi-24s, four of which were delivered at 2020. In 2019 Kazakhstan and Uzbekistan agreed to share their military air bases.

Serbia

Following the break up of the Yugoslav republic, a Special Operations unit of the Serbian Air Force operated two Mi-24Vs that were transferred to the Serbian Police in July 2007. The two Hinds were planned to receive an overhaul and limited upgrade but this was later abandoned.

In December 2019 four of the seven new Mi-35Ms that were ordered were delivered to the Serbian Air Force and Air Defence. They serve along side Gazelle Gama anti-tank helicopters with the 714th Anti-Armour Helicopter Squadron at Ladevci Air Base in central Serbia. They are armed with Spiral-2 anti-tank guided missiles and B8V20-pods containing twenty 80 mm unguided rockets.

Cyprus

The Air Component of the Cypriot National Guard was established in 1987. A member of the European Union, Cyprus operates a squadron of its National Guard equipped with twelve short-wing Mi-35P Hind-F helicopters, which were delivered in 2001 following pilot training in Russia. Operated by the 450th

Helicopter Mira based at Andreas Papandreou, Cypriot National Guard's only air base, one crashed on take-off in 2006 killing the Cypriot pilot and Russian instructor.

The surviving eleven helicopters were overhauled in Russia by the 419 Aircraft Repair Plant at Gorelove, St Petersburg, in 2014. Tasked with defensive, offensive, CSAR and special operations, the Mi-35Ps are normally armed with twenty 80 mm S-8KOM rockets or four 240 mm S-24B rockets. The Cypriot Hind fleet was grounded for several months in 2018 following US and EU sanctions against Russian exporting military equipment, including helicopter spares, but most were returned to service at the end of 2019. In 2023 the Hinds were put up for sale.

Above: One of the Armenian Air Force's Mi-24Vs operated by the 15th Mixed Aviation Regiment based at Yerevan-Erebuni.

Left: An Armenian Air Force Mi-24P, one of fifteen former Soviet Hinds operated by 2 Squadron at Qala Air Base.

The Ukrainian Aviakon Aviation Repair Plant upgraded nine Azerbaijan Air Force Mi-24Ps to SuperHind Mk IV standard in 2020. (Aviakon)

A weapons systems officer's view of an 80 mm rockets being fired from an Azerbaijan Air Force Mi-35M.

The Orsha Aircraft Repair Plant is overhauling the Belarus Air Force's Mi-24V/P fleet. (Orsha)

One of the Kazakh Air and Air Defence Force Mi-24Vs based with the 486th Helicopter Regiment at Zhana-Semei Air Base. (Russian MoD)

A Kazakh Air and Defence Force MV-24V in exercise *Peace Mission 2012,* held at the Chorukh-Dayron training range in northern Tajikistan. (Russian MoD)

Ten short-wing Mi-35Ms are being delivered to the Kazakh Air and Defence Force operating from the 602nd Air Base at Shymkent. (Rostvertol)

Uzbekistan Air and Defence Force Mi-24Ps operated by the 66th Separate Helicopter Regiment based at Chirchik Airbase. (Russan MoD)

One of twelve Cyprus Mi-35P delivered in 2001 and operated by the Cypriot National Guard's 450th Helicopter Mira based at Andreas Papandreou. (Rostvertol)

A bird's-eye view of the pilot and weapon systems officer of a Cypriot National Guard Mi-35P at low level. (Rostvertol)

Cypriot National Guard Mi-35Ps were overhauled in Russia by the 419 Aircraft Repair Plant at Gorelove and given a new camouflage scheme in 2014. (Dirk Jan de Ridder)

Two of the Serbian Air Force's Mi-35Ms displayed with their Spiral-2 anti-tank guided missiles and B8V20-pods. (Serbian MoD)

Serbian Air Force Mi-35M '101' operated by the 714th Anti-Armour Helicopter Squadron at Ladevci Air Base in central Serbia. (Serbian MoD)

Chapter 12

The Army Aviation of the Russian Aerospace Forces

After the dissolution of the Soviet Union, the Russian forces helicopter assets were assigned to the Ground Forces, but on 1 January 2003 they were transferred to the Russian Air Force. However, in 2015 it became the Army Aviation of the Russian Aerospace Forces with structural changes in the organisations control system. Its intended role was to solve operational and tactical tasks during army operations.

The 18th Army Aviation Brigade (AAB) was established in the Eastern Military District (MD) in 2016 stationed in Khabarovsk. The Central MD was supplemented with the 17th AAB at the end of 2017 at Novosibirsk. Each AAB consists of two operational Independent Helicopter Regiments (IHR) equipped with twenty-five attack helicopters, a mix of Mi-35Ms, Mi-28Ns and Ka-52s The Western MD's 15th AAB was stationed at the former naval air airfield in Ostrov while the Southern MD's 16th AAB was formed in Zernograd, Rostov Region. In 2021 the Army Aviation of the Russian Aerospace Forces had more than 200 Hinds in its inventory, which included eighty Mi-35Ms, belonging to Army Aviation Bases in the four Joint Strategic Commands, headquartered in St Petersburg in the Western MD, Rostov-on-Don in the Southern MD, Yekateringburg in the Central MD and Chabarovsk in the Eastern MD.

The Western MD borders NATO member states of Estonia, Latvia, Lithuania and Poland and also controls bases in the Kaliningrad enclave. Two squadrons of Mi-24Ps and Mi-35Ms are assigned to the 549th IHR based at Pushkin and Pribylovo, while a Baltic Fleet Helicopter Squadron operates at the 72nd Aviation Base at Chkalovsk in Kaliningrad with Mi-24VPs. In the Central MD, Hinds are assigned to the 412nd IHR at Chita, the 337th IHR at Novosibirsk, and the 440th IHR at Vyazma-Dvoyevka.

The Southern MD, which borders the Black Sea and Ukraine, has three Army Aviation units: the 37th Composite Aviation Regiment at Simpferopol, the 55th IHR at Korenovsk and the 387th IHR at Budyonnovsk, each with a mix of Mi-24Ps and Mi-35Ms. A Russian Federal National Guard unit, the 685th Independent Composite Aviation Regiment, is equipped with Mi-35Ms based at Kochubeyevskoye. The Russian Border Guard is a military branch of the Federal Security Service (FSB), a successor of the Soviet KGB mainly responsible for internal security of the Russian state. The Army Aviation component of the Eastern MD comprises the 319th IHR at Chernigovka and the 364th IHR at Srednebelaya.

Russia had been a long-time supporter of Syria's president Bashar al-Assad and had been extending military support to his regime since the Syrian civil war began 2011. Following territorial gains by the so-called Islamic State of Iraq and the Levant (ISIL) in 2014, Russian Aerospace Forces began conducting air operations in Syria in September 2015.

Russian Mi-24P helicopters were deployed to the Bassel Al-Assad airport, which became known as Humaymim Air Base, south of the city of Latakia. A total of twelve Mi-24Ps from the 113th IHR in Novosibirsk-Tolmachevo were joined by four new Mi-35Ms drawn from the 55th IHR in Korenovsk in December 2015, the first time the variant had been used in combat. Their initial role was to provide fire support to ground forces using unguided rockets but as the weather deteriorated in the spring of 2016, which restricted their use, this role was taken over by the Mi-28N and Ka-52 attack helicopter, both of which had their baptism of fire Syria.

When Russian president Putin announced a partial withdrawal from Syria in March 2016, Russian helicopters had flown a total of eighty-seven combat missions. However, they were not withdrawn and continued to fly from Humaymim, resulting in the loss of one Mi-35M that was shot down by ISIL east of Palmyra on 8 July 2016, killing the two-man crew, while another was destroyed after being hit by ground fire and making an emergency landing near Huwayis on 3 November. On 31 December 2017, a Russian Mi-24P crashed in Hama province after striking power lines, killing two of the three-man crew.

In September 2019 Russian Aerospace Forces began helicopter patrols from a base at an airport in the north-eastern Syrian city of Qamishli, which was protected by mobile Pantsir-S1 surface-to-air missile systems. Mi-35Ms from the base flew at low level to escort Russian military police convoys near the Syrian-Turkish border. A Russian Mi-35M crashed in Al-Hasakah Governorate in north-east Syria near the Qamishli base injuring the three-man crew on 28 February 2021.

In March 2021 the commander of the Russian Aerospace Forces, Lieutenant General Alexander Titov, indicated that one of the main roles of the Mi-35Ms was to patrol the perimeter of the Humaymim Air Base. At that time there was no sign of the Russian forces withdrawing from Syria.

In addition to the Russian Aerospace Forces and Airborne Forces, three Mi-35MS VIP variants with weather radar, larger windows and equipped with the Vitebsk L370E8 defensive aid suite (DAS), which is now fitted to all Russia military Mi-35Ms, are operated by the Federal Protective Service (FSO), a federal government agency concerned with tasks relating to the protection of high-ranking state officials, including the president of Russia.

However, after carrying extensive military exercises in Belarus, Russia invaded Ukraine on 24 February 2022. Russian Hinds were at the forefront of the attacks on Ukraine targets, although their loss rate was high. Both Mi-24Ps and Mi-35Ms were shot down by Ukrainian MANPADS and after two months they were largely replaced by Ka-52As and Mi-28Ns, which also fell prey to Ukrainian MANPADS supplied by NATO countries.

The Army Aviation of the Russian Aerospace Forces continue to operate a diminishing number of venerable Mi-24V Hind-E helicopters.

An Army Aviation ground crew load an Mi-24P's twin 30 mm GSh-30K cannon with 450 rounds of ammunition. (Russian MoD)

An Mi-24P's ground crew load 80 mm S-8 unguided rockets into its B8V20 underwing launcher pods. (Russian MoD)

Mi-24P '08 Blue' flying over the Pogonovo training area near the Ukraine border. (Russian MoD)

Mi-24P '20 Yellow' lifts off from a snow-covered Torzhok Air Base in 2013. (Alex Beltyukov)

Mi-24P '16 Red' flies low over the Caucasus mountain range during high altitude training by Western Military District pilots. (Russian MoD)

Thumbs up from the weapon systems officer from Mi-24P '16 Red' flying low through a valley in the Caucasus. (Russian MoD)

An Mi-24P hovers above the Caucasus uplands with Mount Ebrus, the highest peak of the Caucasus Mountains, in the background. (Russian MoD)

30 mm cannon shells being ejected as Mi-24P '06 Red' fires its twin GSh-30K gun during live fire exercise at the Mulino training centre. (Russian MoD)

Mi-24P '07 Red' assigned to the 440th Independent Helicopter Regiment at Vyazma-Dvoyevka. (Russian MoD)

A Western Military District Mi-24P '07' Red flies a winter training mission over the snow-covered Smolensk region. (Russian MoD)

Pilot's-eye view from an Mi-24P with another Hind-E during a training mission over Smolensk in the Western Military District. (Russian MoD)

An Mi-24P fires unguided rockets during a live-fire part of exercise *Center 2019* at the Ashuluktraining ground in the southern Orenburg region. (Russian MoD)

A lineup of Mi-24Ps including '17 Red' at Kubinka Air Base as their aircrews prepare for the Victory Day flypast over Moscow in 2019. (Russian MoD)

Mi-24Ps '06 Red' and '25 Red' return to Kubinka Air Base after a rehearsal for the Victory Day flypast in 2019. (Russian MoD)

Mi-24Ps '26' and '29 Yellow' from Tolmachevo Air Base at Novosibirsk in Siberia fly low level in Tajikistan during exercise *Indestructible Brotherhood 2019.* (Russian MoD)

Sporting a freshly applied camouflage scheme, Mi-24P '07 Red' took part in Aviadarts 2021 competition. (Russian MoD)

Mi-24PN '109' with narrow wings and fixed undercarriage of the Mi-35M at the Rostvertol facility in 2013 before the Zarevo III system was fitted. (David Oliver)

Night capable Mi-24PNs equipped with the Zarevo III system were assigned to the 549th IHR at Pribylovo Naval Air Base near St Petersburg. (Russian MoD)

The Mi-35M production line at Rostvertol's facility at Rostov-on-Don in 2013. (David Oliver)

A factory-fresh Mi-35M lifts off from Rostvertol's flight test centre in 2013. (David Oliver)

One of five Mi-35Ms being built for the Russian Federal Security Service at Rostvertol in 2013. (David Oliver)

Ground crews prepare two recently delivered Mi-35Ms carrying four 500-litre external fuel tanks for the Victory Day flypast in May 2015. (Russian MoD)

Mi-35M '34 Red', with Mi-24P '03 Red', flying over Syria prior to it being shot down by ISIL near Palmyra in July 2016, killing the two-man crew. (Russian MoD)

Mi-35M '33 Blue' from the 55th Independent Helicopter Regiment in Korenovsk was based at Tifor in Syria in September 2017. (Russian MoD)

Mi-35Ms '32 Blue' and '40 Blue' took part in Aviadarts 2018 at Dyagilevo Air Base in the Ryazan area. (Russian Helicopters)

Mi-35M '56 Red' with the Vitebsk L370E8 DAS UV sensors in front of the landing gear, belonging to the 549th IHR at Levahovo Air Base near St Petersburg. (Russian MoD)

An Mi-35MS VIP variant with weather radar, larger windows and equipped with the Vitebsk L370E8 DAS operated by the Federal Protective Service. (Russian MoD)